PARTY TIME
GROWING UP IN POLITICS

PARTY TIME

GROWING UP IN POLITICS

JOHNNY FALLON

MERCIER PRESS

WHAT YOU NEED TO READ

Mercier Press
Douglas Village, Cork
www.mercierpress.ie

Trade enquiries to Columba Mercier Distribution,
55a Spruce Avenue, Stillorgan Industrial Park, Blackrock, Dublin

© Johnny Fallon, 2006

1 85635 520 9

10 9 8 7 6 5 4 3 2 1

Mercier Press receives financial assistance from
the Arts Council/An Chomhairle Ealaíon

Printed in Ireland by Colour Books Ltd.

CONTENTS

To our baby Maria,
may you never lose faith.

FOREWORD

As someone who has witnessed the changing nature of Irish politics over the last thirty years, it is refreshing to learn of a young man's passion for the cut and thrust of party politics at a time when interest in Big Brother appears to supersede awareness of current affairs.

Johnny Fallon's account of growing up in a 'Fianna Fáil house' and jumping head first into the maelstrom of Irish political life is an insightful account of life at the coalface of Irish politics All political parties survive, and indeed thrive, on the thousands of volunteers who swear allegiance to an organisation and traipse the highways and byways in the hope of winning votes and getting candidates elected. The approach to the task in hand, whether it be election to the officer board of the local cumann or a seat in Dáil Éireann, remains constant. Total dedication is required and often given in spades. The hours spent at the wheel chauffeuring the favoured candidate to cumann meetings is a lonely and thankless job. Yet, it is only by meeting the local organisation that a full appreciation for the issues that shape the views of the people of Ireland can be garnered. Indeed, some political careers have been built on the back of such endeavours!

Born at time when politics in Ireland was entering the television age, Johnny Fallon captures the passion and unflinching loyalty for the Party leader. Where Kenny Dalglish fits in many young boys' memories, find Charlie Haughey. A local county football or hurling hero is substituted by Albert Reynolds. With such horizons, it is not surprising that the decision of Fianna Fáil to enter coalition government in 1989, takes on such seminal importance. The collapse of Albert Reynolds' government in 1994 causes a funereal trance to descend; a trance so bad that it leaves him blind to a young woman's glad eye.

8

The gallop through a campaign for election to Fianna Fáil's National Executive (the august Committee of Fifteen) provides the reader with a flavour of the commitment that is required of members to reach key positions in a political party. The dedicated are not to be deterred, however. In this case, Johnny is prepared to sacrifice the much valued 'job in the bank' when the question of a conflict with the bank's human resource code is raised.

All political parties rely on volunteers for their lifeblood. This book provides a rare first hand account of such a volunteer. Few outside the political process understand the stresses, strains and headaches that go with positions such as a Constituency Director of Elections or National Executive Representative. At one and the same time, there is pressure from Party Headquarters and the local grassroots. And yet for those who catch the political 'bug', there is little choice. A life of service and utter loyalty awaits. I can only hope that this book encourages one or two more to dip their toes.

P. J. Mara

INTRODUCTION

OK. So first off you are probably asking, who the hell is this guy? Well, the answer is I'm nobody. Nobody in particular anyway. I am just one of the many thousands of Irish people who are born into politics. Family politics is a strong and proud tradition, often berated but never proven wrong. I'm just a cog in that wheel. I have never done anything that changed the world or left my name on the side of a building, at least not officially anyway. I'm one of those people who knocks on your door during a general election, one of those people who hands you a flyer outside a shopping centre, someone who has had their fingers and toes frozen or been soaked to the skin, all in the name of getting a vote. I am simply representative of the many, many people who are involved in Irish political parties.

What I do have, though, is a story to tell, a story of growing up in a world steeped in politics and becoming the nearly thirty-year-old Irish male that I am – a confusing experience at the best of times, but one I can explain, I hope. And at this stage of my life I'm fed up of screaming at the television when people on it annoy me, fed up of not being heard even when I explain my point of view over and over, so here I'm going to put it on the record just for once.

I want people out there to try and understand just how weird it can be growing up with politics, how families and supporters, even though not central to events, are so deeply affected by them. Politics becomes your life, your all-consuming passion.

There are many of us political supporters out there. Few people listen to us. Many laugh at us when we tell them why we believe what we do. Media heads dismiss our opinions as 'blind'. Well, whatever our political perspective, we are people who can see and understand at least as well as those who would like to put us down.

So you're saying, that's all well and good but who wants to read about Fianna Fáil? Look, there's no point beating around the bush here: everyone in Ireland is political. Everyone has a view, even those who tell you 'I don't support anyone, but I hate that party.' Come on, you're just the same as the rest of us, every bit as political. And let's be honest, it's easier to understand people when they're upfront and tell you who and what they stand for. I tell my story from the perspective I know, that of growing up in Fianna Fáil. I know there are others who grew up in Fine Gael and Labour and so on, and believe me their stories are very similar to mine, but there is no point in me trying to tell you their story. No, this story is purely mine, and if it enrages you or makes your blood boil, I can assure you that you have probably done the same to me on more than one occasion. On the other hand, if you are a political person, I'm sure there is much you will understand and relate to here. And if you are not political, perhaps it will make you see just what being in politics involves, and give you an understanding of what makes people like me tick. If you can accept that this is my view, and that for everything I believe there is someone else equally convinced that the opposite is the case, then you might just enjoy this book.

It's give and take. Although we would go through each other for a shortcut in a general election, some of my best friends come from very different political persuasions. This story gives a view from the ground, albeit from my own sometimes biased perspective, but it's also about the respect and understanding that most people in politics have for each other. It's about the love of a political movement. It's about winning and losing, the sheer joy and absolute heartbreak. It's about what makes Ireland great – the rivalry, debate and passion of politics. And I guarantee you that there is one thing this book never does, and that is sit on the fence.

1

BORN TO DARKNESS

In certain rural areas of Ireland people are referred to as being 'born into a political bed'. It's an adage used to describe the poor unfortunate who is unsuspectingly born into a family with a long tradition of serving a political party. It's not the being born part that starts your life-long affliction, of course, but the fact that the child lies down with the political bug, and once bitten finds he's hooked, addicted to a game that as we all know can only end in failure.

When you think about it, there should be some sort of warning about the dangers of political life, but, alas, none has so far been devised, so many embark on this deadly road with the innocence of children.

I am one of those children. Born in December 1976, the last year of the Fine Gael–Labour coalition, just before the Jack Lynch landslide of 1977. I have often wondered if God levels things up politically. I was born into a Fianna Fáil bed; does that mean that some other poor cratur was being gifted unto the Blueshirts at the same time? After all the Christmas number one was 'When a child is born'.

To be fair, I didn't have much involvement in the 1977 election. I can't even say if my parents showed me off to any baby-kissing politician, there are no pictures, and for escaping that trauma I must at least be grateful. They say children can sometimes remember things from inside the womb; well, I don't know how true that is, but I always get an eerie feeling when old archives play the election jingle 'Your Kind of Country'. I'm pretty sure the sticker must have made it onto my cot at some stage and given me hours of wide-eyed wonder.

My parents lived in Dublin at the time. My mother, Gaye Cox, was a pedigree Dub, with uncles who were locked up in Kilmainham in 1916 and rosary beads worn out with prayers for de Valera. She was a trendy young woman, well used to modern city living, but her political roots were never in doubt. Any childish lullabies were always carefully balanced by a final rendition of 'Kevin Barry'. Perhaps I should have realised that there was something slightly wrong with me at this early stage, songs of eighteen-year-old youngsters being hanged didn't seem to bother me a bit. I would drift off, dreaming of the heroic ideal, and never thought of him hanging in ultimate failure; rather, I thought of his glory as he walked to his death, 'softly smiling that old Ireland might be free'. Ah God, it still brings a tear to my eye, thinking of my mother at my bedside singing, and here we are now in a bright new free Ireland. God bless Dev!

My father, Mickey Fallon, had no Dub in him at all – he was a Longford man. The Fallon family had lived around a little corner called the Turlough, straddling the parishes of Cashel and Lanesboro, for as far back as records could find. Even the famine couldn't move them, although they seemed to have had an awkward tendency for having only one son, which doesn't make my task any easier at all. Bad enough to carry your own burdens as a communion-money-grabbing seven-year-old, without having to carry the weight of the dead generations on your shoulders too. The parish of Cashel and village of Newtowncashel is in the very southwest of County Longford, right along the banks of the Shannon, and is about as rural and peaceful a part of Ireland as you could find.

You might wonder how my parents managed to meet, born as they were in different parts of the world. Well, that's a romantic story in itself. My mother was getting tired of waiting for Mr Right to arrive and decided to be a bit more proactive in her approach, so she placed an ad in the penfriends column of *Woman's Way*. My father always bought the magazine for Granny, and as fate would have it he decided to glance through the pages on this occasion. Spotting the ad and figuring that she sounded like a nice girl, he took a gamble and responded. Something about his reply caught my mother's attention and they corresponded for six months before arranging finally to meet. They soon knew it was love, and have been happily married now for over thirty years thanks to Woman's Way, though they always just said a friend introduced them. I always thought it very romantic, certainly beats just bumping into someone after a few pints at the Disco.

My parents moved to Dublin, where Dad worked on the buses. He left behind a GAA team in Cashel that he trained at under fourteen and minors. They went on to win the county championship in 1977. Thinking of it now, 1976–77 must have been the best years of my father's life – a county championship, a son, and the overall majority!

I'm told that when I was born there were precious few phones in Longford, so Dad rang the local shop with the news. The shopkeeper, Chris Rollins, delivered the week's shopping to my grandmother with the tactful note, 'Mickey had a son'. No room in those days for the mother's part in the process – it was the golden age when a man pacing the hall during childbirth was truly appreciated.

Of course, all this self-indulgence is a little unfair to my sister Margarita, who was three years old by the time I turned up and already going off to the cinema to see *The Jungle Book* with her father – but, hey, she can write her own book, this one is all about me.

In 1979-80 my grandparents took ill and Mam and Dad took the decision to move to Longford and build a house there. Sadly, my grandparents died shortly after this, and I must admit I have only fleeting memories of them. My grandparents on my mother's side had died before I ever arrived, my grandmother a few years previously and grandDad – my mother's father – when she was only twelve. That hadn't made for an easy life for her family when she was growing up; there were precious few supports in those days in the new, free Ireland.

I first became aware of politics in the early 1980s, when I started going to school. I remember bumper-stickers and posters being lodged in our house like an arsenal of secret weapons, and the comings and goings of local mandarins. It was a time of controversies, grotesque, unbelievable, bizarre and unprecedented – GUBU for short – and politics and elections were on the television as often as ad breaks. 1982 saw the start of the new Fine Gael–Labour coalition, and my father was so vehement and vociferous in his arguments with Garret Fitzgerald that I thought the television must be a bit like a telephone – certainly Dad roared so he could be heard by the Taoiseach. Anyone who passed by the house during the six o'clock news couldn't fail to hear him either.

Speaking of telephones brings me to another great influence on Irish life in the early 1980s, the radical upgrading of the telephone system. Gone was the disastrous era of waiting years just to have a line installed, and this was all down to the efforts of one far-sighted and progressive minister, a man approaching the status of messiah in the minds of Longford people, Albert Reynolds TD. OK, I know you're going to say I'm biased, and of course I am. Everyone is, in some way, and I'm sure a Blueshirt will reply eventually with a book of his own to balance things up and tell you of the great Louis J. Belton. Ah, God bless him: 'Louis J. all the way!' I remember him showing us how to sing 'Arise and Follow Charlie' after a Longford Association dinner in Dublin many years and many pints later. In fairness, he didn't get the credit he deserved for winning a seat in Longford for Fine Gael at a time when Fianna Fáil was so dominant there; in fact, he was only the second Fine Gael TD ever for the county.

All those lectures my father delivered to the television influenced me, and I often wondered who actually voted for those crazy Blueshirts whose sole ambition in life was to destroy the country and plunge us all into an abyss from which there would be no escape. Of course, I was reminded that people voted for Hitler too, and that if you told enough half-truths some of the people would be bound to believe you. That explanation was good enough for me, and I happily ran outside to be Ronnie Whelan and score the winner in the FA cup final, which we played and replayed most evenings in the garden behind our shed.

But around this time, too, I began to notice that I was different, what the other kids called 'weird'. A freak. I cut photos of Garret Fitzgerald from the newspapers and draped them over my dartboard, and I must say he made a good target. My toy soldiers lined up as political parties, with Fine Gael and Labour as Germans and Japs respectively. My green soldiers were Fianna Fáil to a man. Ah, go on, you've done it yourself ... Well, maybe just me, then.

It was around then, too, that I discovered I had a voice. God help the hapless teacher who inadvertently said something which could be construed as anti-Fianna Fáil. 'I watched television last night as well, Miss,' I would think cunningly, knowing I had the added advantage of my father's running commentary, and that he knew the answer to everything. And still does.

As time went on, I discovered that once a year, at least, I was a god. Copybooks and pencils would fly at me from all corners of Johnny Connor's big yellow school bus as my schoolfriends cadged answers to questions about the budget. No bother getting a seat that morning, no sir. Of course, things would quickly revert to normal a day later.

So, over the years my political edge was cultivated, though I must admit that it wasn't the prettiest time to be growing up. New free Ireland was losing its veneer. Reporters talked of it as a 'failed political entity'. All parties had to shoulder some of the blame for this. Fine Gael's Michael Noonan said national debt would have to rise before the economy could be stabilised, a big mistake, and emigration was seen by all as a natural escape valve for unemployment. In fact, looking back I seemed quite prepared for the idea that I was going to be forced to spend some part of my life abroad looking for work. I would wonder if the Democrats in the United States could use some political advice – they never seemed to win anything – and if there might be an opening for me there.

2

HIGH HOPES AND HOOLIES

1987: the year of my political birth. At ten years of age I was more than old enough to start pulling my weight. I had recently been elected as youth officer of the Fermoyle cumann, the local unit of the Party. Fermoyle was the local National school that I attended and was also the polling station for a catchment area that encompassed part of the parishes of Cashel and Lanesboro.

In every parish and village in Ireland there is a cumann, which looks after the interests of the Party in the area of the local polling booth. The chairman of a local cumann is someone who deserves respect and has authority in political matters. Each cumann sends delegates to the comhairle ceantair (CC), the next level up, which looks after the local electoral district. Such districts can be harder to manage as they bring together many parishes, most of them with long-standing rivalries and very different aims. However, they are joined in the firm belief that their party is right, and despite tearing strips off each other at meetings they try to remain unified outside of it. A comhairle ceantair chairperson is held in much more esteem than his local counterpart, and it can often take years of networking and proving oneself before such an honour is granted to you. Usually it carries the benefits of authority, not just in your local electoral district, but in the Party across the county. It's the recognition factor:

'That's your man, the chairman of the comhairle ceantair out in Ballymahon.'

'Oh, be God aye. I must have a chat with him. He's a good one to know – lot of votes there.'

The ultimate ruling body in a constituency or county is the comhairle Dáil ceantair (CDC). This is where ultimate power is said to lie. These boys plan elections, make major decisions. They

remain in constant contact with Party headquarters. They are close
to the local TD and usually form his backroom team. The chairman
of the CDC is a powerful local figure, someone you hold in a certain
awe. They are second only to the TD in terms of stature, but even
then are often expected to remind a wayward TD that the Party
comes first and his job is to make sure its interests are looked after.
Getting into such a position can often require a lifetime's work –
and there you were, thinking politics was easy to get into, that a TD
was the only one who had to spend time working to get a position.
There is a long apprenticeship, and rising to such heights in the
Party can require as much effort, dedication and political acumen
as becoming a TD.

Each CDC sends one delegate to the árd comhairle or national
executive, who, along with representatives of other groups like
women's or youth bodies, form the overall authority of the Party and
meet with the Taoiseach once a month. They are the ultimate ruling
body in the Party and in theory set policy and make decisions until
the Party Ard Fheis meets. Later on I will explain the workings
of the árd comhairle in more detail. For now it is sufficient just to
see the depth of the Party and to understand why it is impossible
to progress up the ranks unless you are incredibly able politically.
Essentially, while being youth officer of my cumann was really an
entry level cadetship, the fact that it was bestowed on me at ten
years of age showed two things. Firstly, that the rule governing the
age you need to be to hold a position is often ignored, and secondly
that the other members of the cumann held me in enough regard to
actually value some of what I had to say. That's a mighty big honour
when you are only ten and it certainly helped fuel my interest in all
things political.

At home, the record of 'Arise and Follow Charlie' which we
bought at the Árd Fheis blared from our sitting-room during the
weeks of the election campaign, while a larger-than-life poster of
Albert stared out the window at all who passed by, reminding them
of their solemn duty on voting day. As the cumann got canvassing,

I learned about polls, and how they were looking good for Fianna Fáil. I saw how flyers were distributed. I learned how to hang a poster, and all the little tricks that went with it, like the right height to place it so it couldn't be defaced but could still be read by anyone going by. I watched and learned as the whole goddamn show was organised. The night before polling day the Fermoyle cumann always held the final rally of the election in the Peer Inn, Lisnacusha, formerly 'Rakish Paddy's'. The pub is literally in the middle of nowhere, and if you did not know the area there was no way you would ever find it. The Peer Inn was our fortress, and the rallies there were the stuff of legend.

The night of the rally in the Peer I was all decked out in badges and hats and stickers, resplendent in the glory of certain victory in the following day's polls. I left the flyers on the table and accepted the many compliments of the folks around.

'Aren't ya a great little man.'

'Fair play to ya, young Fallon, you're the right man.'

'Are you not running? Sure wouldn't I vote for you myself.'

I noticed two things very early on: men's promises of votes and the success of my political future increased with each pint of Guinness that was consumed; and, secondly, Mammies loved me. Believe me, I have survived for many years and avoided many a tight scrape in life thanks to my ability to woo the Mammies. I love them.

Of course, Albert arrived in at some godforsaken hour in the morning, when I was beginning to get sleepy. I was planted in front of him, looking more like a Fianna Fáil Christmas tree than a functioning ten-year-old, but someone kindly informed him on my behalf that I wanted to become Taoiseach.

'Good man,' says Albert. 'Take my advice: start at the top and work your way down.'

I brushed the sleep from my eyes and tried to make sense of that, and gratefully took the glass of Coke someone gave me and the ensuing burst of hyper-active energy it brought to help me celebrate further.

Polling day. A political volunteer's duties are never done. Polling booths have to be manned, electoral registers checked, party voters visited in case they need a lift. Party volunteers can go over a register and fairly accurately assign every vote in a polling booth down to the last individual, give or take a few. Secret ballot, my arse! Granted it's different in the city, but you would be surprised at how many people actually know the way you vote.

Then the volunteers on duty have to be fed, and God bless the women of the Fermoyle cumann, they were the best feeders in five counties. Stacks of sandwiches, cocktail sausages, chicken nuggets; enough tea to flood China. Hungry work, electioneering.

So, I hear you say, that's all very well but where does a ten-year-old fit in? Surely I got a nice lie-in after the night before? You must be joking! At 9 a.m. I was outside the polling station with my flyers (you could stand a lot closer in those days) catching everyone for a last minute canvass on their way in. Putting on my best pleading face and saying 'Vote for Albert'. Toughest job of the lot, if you ask me. How I envied those inside. I would peer through the window and see them all warm and cosy and full of mirth, drinking their tea and chatting. All I had for company was a bemused-looking cow who stared over the wall opposite, chewing the cud. Still, after one day with me she was the most Fianna Fáil cow that ever grazed the pastures of Ireland.

Cars pulled up, ferrying voters to the polling station, the sound of their heaters blowing as the car door opened, like a devil sent to tempt me. It was a twelve-hour day, you know. Talk about child labour, at least they were paid down the mines. And you know what? It was worth it, if only to observe the pomp and ceremony of the ballot box being sealed at 9 p.m., the presiding officer tying it up, pencils and books all marked and verified slipped inside, the melting of the wax to make the seal. You knew you were at the heart of the most important practice of western civilisation at that moment. After that it's 'Shut up talking, Da, I really wanna get home,' but undoubtedly at such times I felt a bond with my father that nothing else could have given me. Me and Da, driving home, having done our bit for Ireland. To those of you who have never experienced it, I say one up for me; you'll never know how special a feeling that was!

Funnily enough, my father didn't like going to the local count – he felt too cut off from nationwide results when he was there. He much preferred to sit in front of the telly crunching the numbers, analysing results and predicting seats across the country. RTÉ have no concept of the depth of analytical knowledge they are missing – it's found in the living-rooms of local members of all parties right across the country. Can't you just see it now, chief news correspondent Charlie Bird being forced to wander from house to house, talking to farmers, lorry drivers, milkmen and turf cutters about what was happening politically; being made sit and listen and put in his place as to the true depth of his knowledge. No better people to put him right on that score.

I sat at the television all day and observed the results with joy, as it was clear that victory was on its way, only taking a break to eat and play a quick cup final where I was now the Taoiseach who scored the winning Liverpool goal (sorry, Ronnie). As the evening dragged on, I learned the purgatory of counts. They ran late into the night, until at some stage my mother sent me to bed, worn out physically and mentally. Although I was usually a heavy sleeper, somewhere in the wee hours I was woken by the sound of the kitchen light being switched off and the door closing with the kind of soft thud that your teacher would spend hours describing for meaning and significance if it were an act in a play. Footsteps came down the hall and paused for what seemed an eternity outside my bedroom door, then Dad finally poked his head in. I jumped up.

'How did it go?'

'Ah, well,' he said, the disappointment evident in his voice already, 'it's grand. They'll get eighty-one. We won't have the majority, but sure I suppose they'll sort something out.'

I can't remember what I said but I know I went back to bed

with my first taste of that bittersweet feeling known only to Fianna Fáil members. It was a great result, a massive endorsement of our party and our work, and Charlie would be Taoiseach, but still the dream of an outright majority had eluded us when or fingers were actually touching it. I think all Fianna Fáil people have a belief that when that majority finally happens all will be well with the world. Even so, I'd be a happy man heading back to school following my 'election break', because I was going into government. Oh yes, I'd be identifying the Blueshirt kids for some serious treatment now.

You know what, though? Being in government isn't all it's cracked up to be. Sure, you get your chance to implement policy, you wreck the other guy's heads because your people hold the positions of power, and you get to know some very important people. But, on the other hand, all anyone ever does is give out to you. No matter what you do, someone is gonna say it's wrong. If something goes really well, another smart arse is going to make out that it would have happened anyway. Smart arses are usually prone to writing in papers or appearing on television calling themselves experts; they have letters after their names and tell everyone how politics works from the library of Trinity or UCD. Didn't see too many of them freezing their balls off outside the polling station! Lecturing us on politics when they wouldn't find the door into a political meeting, let alone get elected as cumann chairman. Some of those smart arses would have been rightly sorted out had they ever arrived in the Peer Inn. Yes, sir, they'd be told middlin' sweet what's what.

Anyway, feck it, we were in power and we would do what was right for the country. Albert was Minister for Industry and Commerce. I wasn't quite sure what he did but I knew it involved factories and jobs as there was an awful lot of talk about that around Longford. It was a tough time, though. The government made a conscious effort to sort out the economy. Debt was stabilised, but not without harsh cuts. Couldn't people see this was for the good of the country? I thrashed it out with my schoolmaster, Colm Harte, who always drew long political conversations out of me and

started me into debating. I had great admiration for him. He was a
wonderful teacher, who cleverly never let his politics be known, but
I always suspected that deep down he was one of us!

And then the teachers unions prepared flyers saying 'What
chance my child?' which were to be given to kids to bring home
to their parents. Go on the teachers! If ever there was a group that
knew how to play on emotion it was them; they couldn't see an
emotional belt without hitting below it. Hordes of tiny kids arriving
home with big eyes to hand their parents the flyers with that line
on it; many a parent must have wept for hours thinking that little
Johnny or Mary was never going to get an education at all now. But
when the master came to me, I promptly told him that while the
cuts weren't nice it was for the long-term good of the country and
so we agreed with the policy, therefore I wouldn't be bringing any of
these home and didn't want one on my desk. For a few weeks I was
looked up to, not for having a political opinion or for whether I was
right or wrong, but because I had spoken up to the master!

These were the years when the fallacy of opinion polls held sway.
Fianna Fáil just kept going up, sometimes topping the 50 per cent
mark, and considering that 45 per cent delivered a majority, there
was a skip in the step of Party members. And so it was that in 1989
we were back on an election footing, this time combined with the
European elections. Fianna Fáil 'Home and Away, The Best Team'
ran the slogan. The popular Australian soap was reaching its zenith,
so at least the kids noticed the poster, if not their parents.

It was clear from an early stage that the electorate felt that
the election was not necessary and that the polls were misleading.
Our figures kept slipping; it was heartbreaking to watch it happen.
Although I was curious about the whole European thing, there was
no doubt that it was overshadowed by the general election. For me
the election followed the same pattern as before –the fact that I
was now two years older did not alter my status on the political
food chain. But it just wasn't as exciting this time around, and come
the day of the count it was obvious we were going to lose a couple

of seats. There was almost a sense of betrayal after all the promise held out by the polls. Maybe it was a sign of a changing mood, but for the first time I could remember, my father was annoyed with Charlie Haughey for getting it wrong. As for me, no way, I still loved Charlie.

There had been an interesting development over the previous years, the formation of Des O'Malley's party, the Progressive Democrats (PDs). Both my parents used to have time for O'Malley, both thought he could have been leader one day, but he did the unthinkable: he walked out on the Party. One thing was driven home to me during that episode: you may not like something, but you change it from the inside, always. No leaving, no running as an independent, no nonsense like that. You were in the Party and you stayed in it. If you had balls you would stick it out and fight for your party, a bit like that McCreevy fella in Kildare, but whatever else might happen, you don't walk out. My father called the PDs 'Persons Displaced', referring to the fact that it was made up mostly of disgruntled Fianna Fáilers.

The end result was that our house had little time for O'Malley, who was viewed as a bitter little man who betrayed our great party and all the people who worked so hard for it. OK, technically he was thrown out, but the truth was he had brought it upon himself by voting against the Party, so it amounted to the same thing. And then the election result threw up a strange new possibility, an FF–PD coalition. Even though coalition was new to Fianna Fáil and could be seen as ditching a core value, Charlie took the plunge. It didn't cause any great difficulty in our house – you followed the Party and if it took a few turns on the way to its overall aim so be it; that was the reality of politics. However, I do remember going to comhairle ceantair meetings where the move sparked off a storm. The media reported members resigning from the Party over it, but as my father pointed out that made them no better than O'Malley, whom they professed to hate for the same reason. We had no complaints to make in Longford anyway; our man was appointed Minister for Finance and great things were expected to happen locally and nationally as a result.

So began another term in government, which was also to coincide with my entry into secondary school, St Mel's College in Longford. I always wanted to go to St Mel's; it was a school with such tradition, standing head and shoulders above anything else in the region. The attitude there suited me perfectly. There was no school tie or scarf bullshit that went on in private schools. It was very much a public school where the man mattered more than the money, but it was also a place with no inferiority complex: St Mel's was expected to be the best in whatever sphere it competed. The school motto, 'Aemula Virtus', just about summed it up. It was taken from the Latin writer, Lucan, who used it to describe Caesar and his ambitions, it was difficult to translate exactly, due to the nature and multiple meaning of the Roman word 'virtue', however it was usually translated as 'Competitive Spirit'. St Mel's was not afraid to stand toe to toe with anyone on any field, but for the same reason it had nothing pretentious about it, it was a place where all were welcome. It was an exciting time for me, and I noticed many of my new schoolfriends starting to become politically aware, too. Certainly lads from the town were. Granted it was all Guns 'n Roses pro-anarchy teen spirit Metallica stuff, but it was politics nonetheless. I was getting into my metal phase too, and discovering I could turn all the lyrics around to suit my own political standpoint.

You can't win every fight and sometimes you have to pick the right ones. At least that's what my father tried to teach me, but in practice he never shied away from any fight. Around this time, though, he did have one struggle which he got no satisfaction from. Dad, like most CIE workers, was a member of SIPTU. More than that, he was a good trade union man, but he was far from happy that a portion of his union dues went to fund the Labour Party. He fought with the union over it, and they fought back, insisting Labour represented them, but eventually they promised to send forms ... They never came, and in the end my father was forced to give up and accept that it was impossible in those days to stop your money going to the Labour Party. In recent years the unions have become a little more open and do allow their members opt out of the scheme – if they ask to. It's a farcical situation. Why don't they have a form which you request, whereby you can increase your contribution to include a donation to Labour, rather than having to ask to have your contribution stopped? It's not huge money on an individual basis, though it adds up to quite a sum nationally. More than that, it's the principle of the thing. Let's face it, if Fianna Fáil were automatically deducting money from people's salaries under the guise of trade unions there would be uproar and the practice would be outlawed.

Around this time I made my first pilgrimage to the mecca of party politics: the Árd Fheis. The undiluted, all-absorbing, sheer adrenalin rush has never left me. From all over the country we came to gather at the RDS, old folk on walking sticks and crutches, trendy youngsters from the youth wing, Ógra. Some decked out in smart suits, trying desperately to be noticed, while wise old warriors stood swapping strategies in corners – well, either that or complaining about the queue for dinner. In the auditorium, the ever-benevolent Charlie stared down on us all like a colossus. The hall had that eerie sense of anticipation as we waited for the main event, the leader's speech. In those days people got in early to hold the seats at the front, and sat all day listening to 'one, two, testing; one, one, two' as the microphones were made ready. Sure, you could go to workshops, but at least one person had to mind the seats.

The real fun was the myriad of stalls that sold all kinds of stuff to the adoring masses. You could pick up any amount of things, practical stuff like mortgage advice or information on health insurance from the professional bodies' stalls. There were stalls promoting the Irish language – I wasn't great at the old Irish, but sure the stuff was free – while the EU stand offered stickers, tee-shirts, and more information than you could handle. I had enough material for years of school projects from just one visit.

Pride of place went to the Fianna Fáil stall itself. You could buy key rings, pens, cuff-links, ties, umbrellas, sports bags, polo shirts, tee-shirts, sweatshirts, lighters, books, tie-pins, records, posters – you name it, it was there. I was decked out for an entire year after a visit to the Árd Fheis.

I spotted Charlie standing behind a barrier and raced over to get his autograph. He was talking to someone who was bending his ear about a swimming pool, but he reached out and took the card I offered. He stopped when he saw I was handing him a biro. He felt inside his own pocket and then someone from behind handed him a gold Cross pen, with which he proceeded to sign the card and return it to me with a wink and a smile. A lesson I never forgot, though not a word was said: don't settle for just doing something when it can be done with style.

Nothing can compare to the sheer hysteria and adulation which greets the president's address to the Fianna Fáil faithful. I have attended other political gatherings over the years and I have to say it is unique – no other gathering can remotely compare to the raw passion of this event. It's a spectacle to behold. I have often wondered, if someone died in the hall, would anyone notice until the speech was over, such is the trance-like mania that descends on these people for whom Party and country are one. 'Come home with your shield or on it,' as the Spartans used to say. That's how we see it, too.

I will never forget the sheer charisma of Charlie Haughey. He was magnetic. People were drawn to him in an inexplicable way. Never before or since have I met someone with such a powerful presence or able to command such respect and authority. The mood of an entire building could be changed just by the knowledge that he was there. It was unreal. Fair play to you, Charlie. I don't know how you did it but you gave a new definition to the word 'presence', and a degree of hope to all of us who are small in stature that height alone does not make the man.

I was still small and incredibly skinny, but when I had my

head shaved I looked right hard. I also discovered that politics had a hidden advantage. I was known as the authority on Fianna Fáil, and it seemed that being able to say that I knew Albert Reynolds impressed a certain amount of young Longford girls. Well, at least I was different from the normal run of the mill, football or band-member set. I was a curiosity, and girls would wonder 'what was that all about, that political stuff'. Sometimes I played the romantic idealist, sometimes the unscrupulous fixer with no limits to the intrigue I would employ. It all depended on the girl, and perhaps whether it was REM or Guns 'n Roses playing in the background. The downside was that they lost interest soon enough – they just couldn't get as excited about Prime Time as I could. This was a problem that was to remain with me for many years, on the other hand though, once that Miriam O'Callaghan first appeared on Marketplace I knew that was someone I could get very excited about.

But all in all life was pretty good to Johnny Fallon. Politics was sweet; frustrating at times but generally good. Problem was, my view of the world was about to take a sharp fall.

On one of those occasions when I was minding the seats at the Árd Fheis, a man grabbed me by the shoulders, and I turned around to see Brian Lenihan. He was one of the great figures of the Party, and he proceeded to sit and chat to me for a few minutes, seeing me there on my own. It wasn't that condescending adult to child chat either; rather I got the feeling that he was genuinely interested in what I had to say and whether or not I was enjoying the Árd Fheis. I would not forget that moment in a hurry.

Brian was a gentleman. He was also the source of one of the first really painful experiences of my political life, when he ran as Fianna Fáil's man in the presidential election of 1990.

Polls – how I hate them – showed the election to be a foregone conclusion. And why not? Brian was one of Ireland's best-loved politicians and a man who had given many years of dedicated service to his country. Who better to understand the role a president had to play?

28

Once the campaign got underway, I was back in election mode. I went into the station in Longford with my Dad to meet Lenihan as he got off the train to do a walkabout in the town. We met Lenihan shook his hand, walked around town with him, crowds following us with happy faces, whooping and hollering. Life was good.

Driving home my Dad turned to me as I was finishing off my snack box from Luigi's chipper and said, 'Now you can say you shook hands with the president.'

'Yep,' I replied confidently, 'and he can say he shook hands with a skinhead.'

We were that confident. When Mel Donlon, who worked in CIE with my father, asked him what he thought, Dad just said, 'Ah, sure it's over anyway, but I hope that Robinson beats Currie to second place.' Mel agreed. Almost everyone felt that this was the real contest. Fine Gael's Alan Dukes needed their candidate, Austin Currie, to come second if he was to maintain his leadership. Mary Robinson was a solicitor who would have had little in common with ordinary folk like my parents, so normally they wouldn't have much time for her anyway, but the chance of inflicting a defeat on the Blueshirts by driving them into third place would really have put the icing on the cake for us.

But it was all to go horribly, horribly wrong. And it was all a load of codswallop as far as I could see. Lenihan was asked if he had rung the president in 1982, as the Fine Gael government fell, to suggest an alternative government, and Lenihan said 'No', he had not.

Here is what I don't understand. Suppose Lenihan had said 'Yes'. As citizens we are all entitled to ring the president, and surely a president should be made aware that an alternative government could be formed? So the problem seems to be that he said no, and then a smart arse (oh, yes, there's always one) produced a tape on which Lenihan said he did make the call. It was all a technicality, but one which ruined the name of a proud servant and was aimed at hurting our party. There was no forgiveness in our house for that.

My heart ached as the polls started to narrow. I don't remember when exactly it became clear that he wasn't going to have the votes but I certainly remember the siege mentality setting in. On a national level pressure was growing as the PDs started looking for a head. All radios in the house and the car seemed perpetually tuned to Radio One for every vital update. The gravity of those voices on radio, Rodney Rice dropping nuggets of inside information to the masses and the endless hours of debate that followed each new development, heightened the tension as the crisis unfolded. The ad breaks seemed to be there just to help relieve the stress.

The next time I saw Lenihan the atmosphere was worlds apart from his previous visit. All day long the media had been speculating on his future and the possibility of a general election. That evening Lenihan was to arrive in Lanesboro, the nearest small town to my home, and deep into what could be considered Brian's heartland, sitting as it does on the Shannon between Longford and Roscommon. Once again I travelled with my father, and a large crowd had gathered outside the parish hall by the time we arrived in Lanesboro. Cigarettes were being smoked like they were going out of fashion. Men with faces flushed from high blood pressure, looking like they might explode at any minute, stomped on the footpath grumbling about the injustice of it all. Women stood there menacingly rocking children in their prams, simmering under the surface and ready to let fly at anyone who might upset Brian when he arrived. It wasn't the place to be if you were from the national media, and granted not too many seemed to turn up, or if they did they stayed well hidden.

Councillor Eugene Murphy from Roscommon approached my father and some others and said, 'Right, lads, remember when he gets off, "No Resignation!" Shout it!'

The men didn't need any encouragement. 'No bloody nothing,' said my father. 'We're not going to be made answer to a shower of go-boys and turncoats.'

There was a mood among the members that had been missing

in the general election, a fighting spirit. The blood was high in Fianna Fáil and all we wanted now was the go-ahead to drive the heathens into the Shannon that very night. Many felt that a general election was coming, too. 'Charlie won't dump Brian,' they said, 'Charlie won't shy away from the fight.' Fianna Fáil backs were to the wall, and if I had learned one thing by then it was that at moments like this the Party was at its most dangerous. In this environment, holidays would be cancelled, time taken off work, and twice as much canvassing done in a fit of pure rage. All we wanted was the word from Dublin …

Lenihan arrived on his bus. The crowd cheered uproariously as he came down the steps, and someone told him he was among his own now. The amazing thing about Lenihan was the loyalty and love that all members had for him; it was like everyone felt that they owed it to him personally. Even the children of the local Fine Gael councillor were there to get an autograph. This was a sign of things to come for Fine Gael – Currie's campaign was bombing – while those who couldn't identify with Robinson's 'Come dance with me' approach were siding up to Lenihan's man-in-the-street campaign. There were more than a few for whom a liberal solicitor dancing around Ireland was a jig too far.

The speeches that night were defiant, Lenihan and Reynolds side by side, body language saying 'not an inch'. After the rally Lenihan moved on into Roscommon and down to Athlone. When Dad and I went home we sat with Mam, who, God bless her, had the dinner ready (hungry work all that rallying) and recounted the news we had missed while we were out. For the first time in several days we actually had a feeling that this could be turned around, but as events played out the following day, it became apparent that all was not well. In the end my father, mother and I sat in silence, staring at the ground, when the news finally broke.

'A letter was sent by the Taoiseach to Mr Lenihan asking him to resign. When Mr Lenihan refused, the Taoiseach had no option but to sack him.'

It was a cruel blow. For once, I really felt that politics was a waste of time. How could this be the reward for years of service? Was this the thanks you got from the people? On the other hand, part of me wanted to be more involved. Brimming with the confidence of an almost fourteen-year-old, I was sure that I could fix it if I were there, I could make people listen. Whatever my doubts about politics, one thing was clear: my faith in Charlie was seriously dented. I felt he let us down. I have often thought since that this was a bigger turning point in Haughey's career as leader than many realised. It was the first time he publicly shied away from a fight, and members quickly began to doubt his nerve and his loyalty.

But the fight would continue, we would do whatever it took, even though you could see that the Party which had had such vigour only a night or two before was now visibly shell-shocked and weakened. Political correspondent Seán Duignan once said that the most memorable interview he ever did was with Lenihan, when he looked straight into the camera and made an impassioned plea to the Irish people. You're not wrong there, Diggy. There were tears in our eyes as we watched Brian, the man who conquered a liver transplant, the man who was for years a faithful servant to Ireland, the man with the interest of the people at heart, and he was begging the people to listen. Not a dry eye in the house, no, but seething anger at how this could have come to pass. My father wrung his hands and raged at Blueshirt plots, agenda-driven media and those 'cowardly rats' in the PDs. My mother, probably knowing what's best, reached for the rosary beads above the fire that night, and we beat it out with all our might, imploring the Blessed Virgin and all the angels and saints to help Brian. I think my mother was more worried for his health than she was his career; she just kept saying, 'This will break his heart, this will kill him.'

Olivia O'Leary chaired the television debate between the candidates and for the first time Robinson started to stick the knife into Lenihan. The Late Late Show had a special programme with all the candidates. Brian was always going to come across best; he was that type of guy. Robinson's campaign managers, Eoghan Harris and Fergus Finlay, differed over the show and the approach she should take, and it proved a disaster for Robinson, who appeared cold beside Lenihan's warm nature. Although she had remained commendably aloof from the crisis up until the end of the campaign, she got stuck in now, but this only served to ensure that many Fianna Fáil people like my family could never, ever forgive her, or even come to like her, after her performance that night. She even ended up questioning Gay Byrne's professionalism, attacking him during the ad break. Gaybo, being well experienced at the game, made her comments and complaints public as soon as the show came back on air.

The sympathy vote was kicking in, our polls were looking better, we still had a chance – even known Blueshirts were wearing Lenihan stickers – but it was too little too late for Brian. On polling day my routine was the same as ever, although such was the positive consensus about Lenihan in our polling booth that I was granted the honour of being allowed stand inside the hall door, which at least meant I would not be wet and freezing standing outside in the miserable weather. It was not strictly within the rules, but no one was going to complain.

Lenihan was the most popular candidate, easily outstripping both of his rivals on first preference votes. However, a pact between Fine Gael and Labour meant that when Currie was eliminated Robinson narrowly overtook him, and won the presidency with just over 80,000 votes in the final difference from a total poll of well over 1.5 million.

I returned to school again, wounded but not beaten, and faced down any teenage abuse with pride. To a teacher who mentioned that I must be upset at losing, I stared back and said simply, 'I'd rather lose with Lenihan than win with the likes of the others.'

I'd made my point, and besides I had other matters to attend to, like the fact that at the time I was on a very rare goal-scoring streak in schoolyard soccer, and needed to get a note through the high security at the convent to tell a young wan why I had been completely uncontactable for over a week due to my critical involvement in national affairs of state, or something to that effect. She bought it long enough to share a bag of Luigi's chips, and a day or two later said goodbye. I think I wrote a song about it, but as my rock star/Taoiseach career seem to be going the same way as my footballer/Taoiseach career, it never went any further.

To be honest, my education wasn't going all that well either. It wasn't just the politics taking me away, I had also begun to suffer allergies to just about everything, and missed more days in school that year than I attended. I got a deplorable report, but consoled myself with the thought that, despite the poor results, most teachers said that I seemed to be a pretty nice and pleasant guy. It was enough to get me elected, so I was happy to settle for that.

Politics has a habit of always having a crisis in the months of October and November, which is pretty awful when you are at school. Nowadays, of course, we seem to have settled in to long-term governments and summer elections, so a bit of that buzz is gone. The cut-and-thrust edge and battle readiness doesn't appear to be there, though mark my words it will return! But this was 1991 so a crisis turned up on schedule. And this time it was closer to home.

Throughout the summer there had been much talk of when Haughey would finally step aside. The mood was gathering that he should go, but there was a consensus that he should do it in his own time. Then he went and frightened the bejaysus out of us all by remarking that Chinese leaders went on until their nineties! Jovial it may have been, but there was no sign that Haughey had any particular timetable in mind.

3

LONGFORD LEADER

My home village of Newtowncashel is the tidiest village in Ireland. When it comes to Tidy Towns we are the experts. Ardagh in Longford won the award as well and, yes, other villages have won it from time to time, but no village has been as consistent for so long, ending up in the top couple of villages every single year. That's some achievement, and so here and now, for once and for all, I am claiming the award for my parish for all time. We are incredibly proud of our record, and the work of all those involved with the Tidy Towns, back home.

It so happened that the Tidy Towns committee was having a presentation in the parish hall in Cashel in November 1991, with finance minister Albert Reynolds in attendance. As fate would have it, just as he was making his way there news started to break that Seán Power, Noel Dempsey and a couple of other youngsters in the parliamentary party (I was nearly fifteen at this stage) were tabling a motion of no confidence in C. J. Haughey. Albert was seen as a likely successor and everyone was wondering if he would take the plunge. He didn't give too much away at the meeting in Cashel but there was something unsettling in his words. His speech seemed to go more deeply to the heart of volunteering and the ethic of good work than the meeting merited, as if he were hinting at a bigger issue. I mean it was just a tidy towns presentation after all.

Afterwards the local party gathered closely around him. I can still see Albert outside 'the Hill', bedecked in his long overcoat, shrugging his shoulders repeatedly and making quick glances all around the street, the way he always did when something major was distracting him. 'We'll have to see,' he kept saying, then off he went in the ministerial Merc in that devil-may-care style, but going home in our Ford Fiesta we were all agreed that Albert had not been himself. He looked like he was ready for the fight. We braced ourselves.

Word came through eventually that Reynolds was backing the motion and the split was complete. We all had to trust Albert and presume he knew best. Every day the papers offered breakdowns of who would vote what way in the motion. Then there was the question of whether the ballot would be open or secret; everyone knew Charlie would win an open vote. They were a traumatic few days, and for the first time I was not on the leader's side, but it didn't bother me. I realised that I truly believed in Albert. It wasn't just the Party thing, I believed in a way I never had before and never have since. That's what it is to have grown up in the vicinity of such a huge political figure, I suppose.

Haughey won the vote. The damage that did was irreparable, and although we would never consider leaving the Party or any non-sense like that, our love affair with Haughey was well and truly over. We had little time for him now. I can remember my father raging in the middle of the kitchen floor about Haughey and 'who did he think he was? He would be nothing if it wasn't for Fianna Fáil.' I actually tore up an old Charlie poster, before wishing once again that I was there because I knew I could make the difference. Ah, yes, the God-given confidence of the Fianna Fáil youth!

Albert was sacked. I spent hours in my room listening to Guns 'n Roses, pacing around trying to lose my anger after watching a 'shower of gurriers' (Dad again) banging on Senator Eddie Bohan's car as he drove Albert out of Leinster House. They had the audacity to start singing 'Albert in a Lada' as they thumped the car. Oh, if we had known then what we know now, those people would have stayed very, very quiet.

The next morning I lay in bed listening to the radio, some DJ on 2FM played 'We're so sorry, Uncle Albert'. What had become of bright, new, free Ireland? Last year, Brian; this year, Albert. Like the 'host of fleet-foot men' who were too late to save Roddy McCorley, all we did was in vain.

The next few months were a novelty at school. I think I taught everyone a lesson about political cut and thrust as they watched this once loyal Haugheyite round on the leader for his treatment of Albert. I made no secret of the fact that I wanted Haughey gone, but also pointed out that I would still serve Fianna Fáil, and while Charlie was leader I would live with it even if I didn't like it, because loyalty to the Party was paramount. Some teachers and students pointed out that this must be a very sore point for me, and it was then I discovered that it wasn't really – growing up in the Party had hardened me. I found I was able to distance myself and wasn't bogged down by moral baggage and problems with conscience. Real politics has no room for them, and anyway moves too fast: indecision is what's punished. In Albert's words, 'the paralysis of analysis'. It was also true that what had probably angered us was not so much Haughey as his supporters. We could never have imagined carrying on in the same abusive manner outside the Dáil that they had.

Albert was welcomed back to Longford with open arms. A huge crowd gathered in the Longford Arms Hotel to greet him. I was there in the front row. Anyone who looks back on the news footage of Albert entering the room will see me straight in front of them, middle of the screen, standing up in my St Mel's uniform. A few minutes of fame that made me a school celebrity for a few hours, and I clung to such moments like gold dust. Albert was presented with a piece of bog oak in the shape of a flame to signify the 'flame that Albert had lit across the country'. Big Ned 'the county' Reilly, the father of Longford Fianna Fáil, a man who seemed to me to be always old, a man who had been there with Dev, stood on the podium and gave the speech of his life, saying how proud he was and hailing Albert as the 'Taoiseach in waiting'. My heart was pounding. 'We'd die for ya, Albert'! We lived off the memory of that night for weeks.

But if weeks are a long time in politics, months are an eternity. Once the media circus passed on we were all left wondering, what now? Charlie settled back to normal and life continued as before. Dad talking about work, Mam redecorating parts of the house, my sister at college in Dublin and me worrying about Christmas results from school. Politics was a world away and already it seemed people were forgetting Albert.

Ballymahon comhairle ceantair was having a meeting in early 1992. Me, Mam and Dad were all on our way in the car and for once the radio wasn't on. Don't ask me why, maybe we just didn't like the news anymore, but it was certainly unusual. We were actually driving along wondering if Albert had 'shot his bolt' and if his chance to be leader was passing him by. When we arrived at the courthouse in Ballymahon, where the meeting was to be held, we could see there was a bit of excitement. Despite the cold night people were milling around outside. As we went into the meeting people began telling us that Seán Doherty, the former Minister for Justice, was on a talk show with Shay Healy called *Nighthawks*, and he was about to say that Haughey knew all about the phone-tapping back in the early 1980s. I never watched *Nighthawks* and thought it a terrible format for a chat show but this ensured the programme would live long in my memory. We waited with baited breath for Albert's arrival. It was the comhairle ceantair's AGM but no one cared about that; we wanted to know what this news meant for Albert. He arrived in a flurry of excitement, people pressing him from all sides. When he spoke, two things were obvious. First, he wanted everyone to keep calm about it; and, second, he wanted to distance himself from that night's revelation.

'I don't know what this means,' he insisted. 'We'll have to wait and see. It might do as much harm as good. I'll have to hear what was said and we will take it from there.'

But we knew. Albert was never indecisive. He knew exactly what he was going to do, and as we all shook his hand and chatted to him you could see a sparkle in his eye. The politician in him smelled blood. Reynolds had the ball right in front of goal, the 'keeper had slipped, and it was up to him to bury it.

I was in school when Haughey officially resigned; I was first onto the mini-bus where Maggie Kilbride, the owner and driver, gave me the news. We both agreed that it was sad to see Haughey go after all, and that he had been a good leader, but nothing could hide the elation we felt knowing that Albert was now the front runner.

My English teacher, and my complete political opposite, Tiernan Dolan, ran a competition for a project in which we would follow the course of the leadership contest. We both had a deep respect for each other, even if we could never agree politically: he was a great teacher who went far beyond the bounds of simply teaching English. For me, winning the competition was a matter of pride. The awkward thing was that it could challenge my position as the most politically adept student in the school. Not that there were many clamouring to take away my crown, they were happy to leave it to me generally, but the prize of £5 could bring all sorts out of the woodwork and these would have to be put firmly in their place. I put in the work, the task was done, and I claimed my prize, my position safe. Now all I had to do was hang around outside the cathedral gate long enough to find some young wan who would help me spend the prize money – that kind of cash could even fund a trip to the cinema.

But the leadership contest wasn't all plain sailing. Firstly, Mary O'Rourke, who was also a minister and represented our neighbouring county of Westmeath, said she would stand. OK, there was no love lost between her and Longford Fianna Fáil, but what the hell was she playing at? Every lunch break I walked up to Dad's car at CIE to eat my snack box from Luigi's and hear the news. Dad was furious with O'Rourke. 'She hasn't a hope. Pure bloody messin',' he concluded. Michael Woods, another front bench minister, stood as well, but we reckoned Albert could take him. Ned 'the county' Reilly said publicly that Albert and Bertie was his 'dream ticket', and the media jumped on the phrase. But it all depended on what Bertie Ahern would do. Bertie was the leading Fianna Fáil figure in Dublin after Haughey and represented the only real challenge to

Albert. Many people in Longford did the sums and all were fairly confident that, even if Bertie ran, Albert would have the numbers, but it would have been very divisive for the Party. In the end Bertie decided to back Albert and history was made; the vote was the biggest ever margin of victory in a Fianna Fáil leadership contest. Oh, the rejoicing, the sheer unbridled joy of it all. Big Jim Tunney, chairman of the parliamentary party at the time, coming out to give the result, and as everyone cheered telling them 'It's not a county final you're at!' Ah, feck ya, rain on someone else's parade. We may be boggers but we're the masters now. Bloody hell, a county gets its first ever Taoiseach and they don't want us to be excited? We were high with excitement. Bennie Reid, the architect of so many of Longford Fianna Fáil's battle plans, had tears in his eyes. The legendary senator, Mickey Doherty, looked like a man who had just passed through the gates of heaven rather than the gates of Leinster House – and maybe he had, even his dodgy hip seemed not to bother him any more!

The day Albert was to be elected Taoiseach, there was half the county Longford travelling up to Dáil Éireann to witness the historic event. What a day, I'll never forget it. Bright new free Ireland was back! We drove up that morning, parking in the Setanta car park just down from Leinster House – my poor father nearly had a heart attack when he saw the rates they were charging! For all my involvement in politics, this would be the first time I set foot inside Leinster House, and that in itself was memorable. I was old enough to appreciate it, too. Everyone was outside the gates. Men in their best suits, women dripping in gold jewellery, and one poor soul there to say farewell to Charlie, fair play to him. Where was the crowd who jeered Albert a few months before? Oh, how we would have loved them to show up; nothing like a good scrap out side the gates of the national parliament.

But all was not well. We couldn't get past the bloody gates. Mickey Doherty was in desperate negotiations but someone some-where was stopping the crowd getting in.

'Charlie doesn't want us!' someone shouted.

'We'll show him who's wanted!'

The crowd got agitated. Was this Haughey's last stand, an attempt to stop us seeing Albert elected? Jaysus, I thought, there is going to be a riot any minute. Then Mickey did it, got us all into the foyer, but told us we needed to find a TD to get us into the public gallery. Mayhem ensued. People grabbed every TD and senator they could find, each one could get two in, and TDs ran like hunted animals from the swarming masses as the stewards struggled to maintain decorum in the house. There were many great stories of how people got in. In scenes reminiscent of the Titanic, mothers and children had to be separated, my mother selflessly leaving Dad and me go in on Noel Treacy's ticket, with strict instructions to my father to mind me. The Galway TD seemed like a vision from god when he produced those passes for us. I looked back at my mother standing alone and wondered when I'd see her again. Lord, the heartbreak! Another member of the Fermoyle cumann, Mary Hurson, practically rugby tackled Des O'Malley on the stairs and demanded he get her in. Des, sensing the mood, duly obliged – you didn't want to get on the wrong side of this crazy Longford crowd. Bobby Molloy of the Progressive Democrats was cornered and gave his passes up; so did Louis Belton of Fine Gael, who did it quite joyfully. TDs were in danger of being lifted up by the ankles and shook until those precious passes fell from their pockets. In the end everyone was crammed in, everyone, that is, except my mother. Standing alone on the stairs, now quiet and lonely, she saw Albert approaching, ready to enter the Dáil.

She approached the new leader and was pushed back by the men in suits, the handlers surrounding him, but being small she squeezed through until Albert spotted her. He looked up from the papers he was reading as he walked and grabbed her hand. 'Albert, I can't get in!' she cried, with a tear in her eye. Albert looked flustered; this was all he needed now.

'I don't have any passes,' he said, but seeing her crestfallen he stopped. 'Look, go back to the office of the captain of the guard. Tell him I sent you and he's to give you the Reynolds' family ticket.'

My mother raced off and confidently told this important looking captain what Albert had said. The man laughed.

'I'm sorry, but I really can't give it to you,' he said. 'You could be anyone, and it's more than my job is worth if I give away that ticket, not without getting the order myself.'

'It will be more than your job is worth if you don't give it to me,' my mother told him.

Just then Donie Cassidy marched in. 'Howaya doin', Mrs Fallon,' he said. 'What's the problem?' The story was laid out before him. 'Oh, Jaysus, give her the ticket. If she says it's true then it is,' Senator Cassidy said. 'I know the Fermoyle cumann well'.

The ticket was handed over and in she came. My family were reunited in a gallery creaking with the crowd crammed into it. Albert's family arrived late (I hoped that had nothing to do with my mother) and sat just in front of us. Albert glanced up, smiling and looking at his watch.

Then came the speeches, farewells to Charlie and a few barbed comments at the incoming Albert as part of the debate. It was so hot in the gallery you couldn't breathe. It was exciting, too, but then Proinsias de Rossa got to his feet and seemed to go on forever. I began to feel weak. My vision started to blur as I tried to focus on Albert – I really should have had my breakfast! My mother took me outside to catch my breath, though getting through the crowd pressed in on all sides of the gallery was a damn difficult task. I cursed my luck, sure I was going to miss it all, but after a few minutes I felt OK. We went back in, and I nearly got sick again when I opened the door to hear de Rossa still droning on. I wouldn't mind if there was a chance that he could defeat the government, but there wasn't. Get on with it, I'm starving to death here! Some of these politicians have no consideration, trying to get a few lines into the paper just so they could say they said something. This was our day, not theirs!

Finally the vote was called. Albert was duly elected and moved from the backbenches to the Taoiseach's chair. What a moment. Then he was off to get his seal from the president and would come back to the Dáil to announce his cabinet in the afternoon session.

When he returned there were no problems getting in. The guard had changed; a new force was in the ascendancy. We were going out to visit my sister, who was studying in the Botanic Gardens at the time. You will notice that she has been absent from many of these stories, but although her politics were never in doubt, she wasn't into being involved the way the rest of us were. Fianna Fáil by birth, yes, but she didn't want to spend her life chasing it like the rest of us. Maybe she was right.

In the meantime, Albert announced his cabinet, a move that earned him the name the Longford Slasher. Half the cabinet found themselves demoted. People like Mary O'Rourke, Gerry 'don't do it Albert' Collins and Ray Burke. Big names. This was a huge move. Reynolds was bringing in a completely new team, one which would be very much his own. Even my father couldn't believe it and was worried that this purge would come back to haunt our new leader. For now, we weren't going to worry about it. Albert had already proved that he knew best.

His homecoming to Longford was a momentous occasion. Bonfires were lit on the Dublin road approaching the town, the main street was closed to traffic and thronged with people ready to greet the new Taoiseach long before he arrived. Half the county must have been on the street that night; nothing like it had ever been seen before. Everyone I knew from school was hanging around, too, with a new-found interest in things political. The speeches were proud and exuberant, and Albert himself couldn't hide the elation and gratitude in his voice. It was one of the few times that I saw him cry, when he was thanking everyone for their support after his wife, Kathleen, had been diagnosed with cancer. It was always plain to see that Albert was crazy about her, and indeed she was hugely liked and admired in Longford in general. She is such a homely, motherly and yet charming and stylish woman that there is absolutely nothing that one could dislike about Kathleen, and there are not many people you can say that about.

As for heading back to school, for once in my life I couldn't wait! For weeks, I walked around like the cat that got the cream. I was set for greatness – how could my life be anything other than hugely successful now that I knew the Taoiseach? By any reckoning, he should knock ten years out of it, and I should be well part of the political establishment by then. With no end to the possibilities that lay before me, the fact that I had the junior certificate fast approaching and not a tap of study done didn't bother me a bit. I was cruising. Myself, and my best friends, Mick Lennon and Ciarán McGuinness were picking up a handy few bob playing traditional music in the Misty Midlands pub every Tuesday night. I was also busy pulling strings with our PE teacher Declan Rowley to ensure that our class got to go to Tourmakeady in Mayo for an adventure weekend. My standing among my peers was on the up, and I didn't take any offence at being nicknamed 'Albert' by teachers as well as students.

The Árd Fheis that year was the best craic ever. Longford people strutted around as if they owned the RDS, telling stewards what to do with themselves if they offended them: 'Right, that's it! I'm reporting you to the Taoiseach.' The giant portrait of Charlie was replaced by an even bigger one of Albert; his image dominated proceedings. Once again we were right up at the front, rows of Longford people. Charlie Haughey came onto the stage and the crowd rose to their feet whooping and cheering. Even though Charlie was no longer leader, it was clear that people still loved him. It seemed to send a message to us, we knew Albert had to get a bigger cheer when he arrived on stage. I was trained at chanting at the St Mel's football matches, and was more than up for it. And when Albert entered, we lifted the roof, standing up on the chairs, stamping our feet, Noel Hanlon, chairman of Aer Rianta and the VHI, behind me beatin' the head off me with a rolled-up newspaper in his excitement. Every time it quietened at all we rapped the seats and started the ovation again. I had welts on my hands from the clapping. My father was roaring as loud as he ever did at football matches, tears rolling out the sides of his eyes, although he said that was from the lights. My mother stood entranced, waving furiously at the podium. God save Ireland!

We got to our feet time and time again throughout our new leader's speech. At one point Albert said a *cúpla focal as Gaeilge*, and we jumped to our feet again. This time the television camera caught me leaping up, and everyone at school must have seen it because I never lived it down. 'There was Fallon leppin', and him with not a word of Irish in his head!' What was worse was that the *Léargas* programme on RTE used that clip in the intro to their show that season, so it was repeated over and over every week on national television, just to remind all and sundry of my antics in case they should forget. Pity it didn't get me any extra credit points in the junior cert! Still, it was something to spout at the disco anyway. 'Yeah, yeah, I'm the guy from the *Léargas* intro, you might have seen me.'

Politics never gives you much time to rest, and it's no respecter of exams either. The Maastricht Treaty referendum was on its way and falling right in the middle of the junior cert. There was work to be done. I breezed into each of the exams as if there were far more important things in life, which there were. The referendum itself was on the same day as my mechanical drawing exam, a subject I hated with a passion. I showed such a lack of interest in it that the teacher, Mr Flynn, finally gave up on me, and would sit down and talk politics instead. I sold him more than a few tickets for functions and raffles while we were at it.

I was outside the polling booth on a beautiful summer's day, wearing a 'Go with Europe – Grow with Europe' teeshirt, when my sister arrived over with my mother to bring me into town to sit the afternoon exam. I was raging. I had figured a nice day outside in the sun could get me some mean tan lines, while I was at it, and this might improve my recent poor run of form with the girls. But I was hauled off and dropped outside the school. As I got out of the car, my mother said she was going to do the shopping, and we would meet later. I told her not to be too long. 'What?' she said. 'You have a three-hour exam.'

'Ma, have you no sense? This is a fail anyway. I'm not wastin' time staring up at the map of Ireland, when the whole future of Europe is hanging in the balance.' I wasn't lying either. After those crazy Danes rejected the treaty, it was down to Ireland to get Europe back on track. So I went into the exam, the lads laughing when they saw me, took my papers and wrote my name at the top like we were supposed to. I glanced at the questions and not a single one made sense; I might as well have stumbled into an exam in Hebrew. OK, I thought, looking at the clock, still time to catch a few votes. I proceeded to draw an ellipse by the concentric circle method, the only thing I was ever able to do in mechanical drawing, and once that was finished I asked for my envelope. The supervisor looked shocked but duly obliged. As I handed it back, he looked at me and said, 'You must be very good at this.'

'Oh, yeah, sure,' I said. 'I should have done honours.'

With that, I walked back into the sunshine, handed out a few leaflets outside the cathedral so my mother would think I spent at least an hour in the exam, then headed back to the car and back to my post.

The result was an overwhelming 'yes', nearly three to one in favour. Albert's first electoral test, passed with flying colours, easy one though it was. We were soaring high in the opinion polls too, and then up pops Des O'Malley to give his evidence at the beef tribunal, were he severely criticised Albert. In the end, Albert, who normally guarded his good name with a vengeance, didn't seem to pay much heed, and simply said he would have his time to give evidence. Nonetheless, O'Malley's little tribunal tirade didn't go unnoticed in our house. If ever there was a man with great potential, but who knew how to make himself unpopular, it was O'Malley. Yes, sir. Every time you started to think the guy might be OK he jumped on your back and tried to strangle you, like Gollum from *Lord of the Rings*.

Guns 'n Roses played Slane castle that summer, 1992, and off I went with the savages and the insane. It was a hot, hot summer's day and a brilliant concert, all the lads up front hoping Axl Rose would do a crowd dive and they could kick the crap out of him – not much hero worship here! Still, a legend of a day all the same. OK, I didn't go for anti-government lyrics, but even that could be made to suit my needs.

Summer that year was beautiful and I took full advantage of it. During term, I'd dated the best-looking girl in the convent for a short while, which seriously improved my reputation, and over the summer the family up the road, the Dowds, had a French student who was the object of my affections for all the time she stayed. Life was certainly looking up!

4

HEARTLANDS

When my parents went on holidays in August, Margarita and I had a great house party, and the weekend they were arriving home Mick and Ciarán rang me to head off to the fleadh cheoil in Clonmel. OK, Mam and Dad would just have to wait until they were home to find out; I was going. The thought of getting away completely unsupervised to what was by all accounts Ireland's greatest drinking session was just far too tempting. It turned out to be one of those rare times when for an entire weekend (with the exception of chatting up a girl) I totally forgot about politics. We travelled down on Fabian Walsh's minibus, with some of the crowd from Longford Comhaltas Ceoltóirí Éireann. Being older than us, they all sensibly headed to B&Bs. We were dropped at the campsite in Clonmel rugby club. Three fellas in a two-man tent, we had to get in one at a time, Mick lying the opposite way to myself and Ciaran, our faces pressed against the tent wall and his head out the tent flap. Wild craic; if you turned you'd probably pull the tent down.

We headed into the pub at 8 p.m. and played a few tunes – easy going, you might say, but an entirely different matter when you staggered back to the tent at 8 a.m. the next morning with blisters the size of bodhráns on your fingers, mumbling a few disoriented words about being 'back home in Derry' and wrestling with some-one's feet through the sleeping bag. Waking up a few hours later, and ready to split someone for a bacon double cheeseburger, it was tough going realising that your only source of income was busking and you were gonna have to do an hour of it just to buy lunch. You know what pain is then. The craic might be ninety in the Isle of Man but in Clonmel it came at a price.

Still, by evening your head starts to clear, you put a few plasters over the blisters and you feel like a new man. You kick off a few tunes and suddenly the man behind the bar is lining up a rake of pints to keep ya: 'Forget your age, garsún.' Oh yeah! Eyeing the young wans that just sat over in the corner, closing your eyes as you play and acting all artistic and talented like. If you get a smile you know they will be putty in your hands; now all ya need is a slow air or a sad come-all-ye to show your emotional side. Next thing you know it's eight o'clock in the morning again, there's not a woman in sight and all you're hugging is an accordion case. Well, that's the fleadh cheoil for ya! Proud parents lugging seven-year-olds around burdened with violin cases on their backs. Teenagers watching every finger movement of legendary musicians like Joe Burke, trying to learn tips and tricks from his years of experience. Arty-farty types sitting around discussing the impact of Irish music and its role in the development of different genres like bluegrass. Hardened drinkers who could have been big if it wasn't for their commitment to Uncle Arthur. Aonghus McAnally (of yellow and orange suit, *Anything Goes* fame) wandering the streets with a film crew, like a god as musicians battled to get their few minutes of fame or, better still, be pictured beating out a tune with some of the great and good. I was just happy to be sitting on someone's pot-plant with my choc-ice, to be honest.

Yes, the summer of 1992 came to a very sweet close, and it was back to school in September, now in my senior years and the in-evitability of those junior certificate results fast approaching. I was becoming anxious about having assured my parents that everything was fine with my studies! When they arrived, the results weren't all that bad, though. OK, mechanical drawing was a fail, but even there I got an E, so apparently for writing my name and drawing a circle that wasn't even asked for I possibly got around 30 per cent or so. I had done honours science for the laugh – in three years I had never passed an exam, and I only took it because I knew that the teacher, Don Murphy, who was a good sport, would despair at the sheer audacity of it. I ended up getting a C. I was very happy with the rest of my subjects and I think my parents were too, convinced now that

I had been telling the truth after all. Phew! That was a close one.

As winter came on, politics added a twist to the tale once again. The beef tribunal was one of the more dramatic events in Irish politics in the late 1980s and early 1990s so I will try summarise it as best I can and to explain the position as we saw it on the ground, but it is worth remembering that the beef tribunal itself could fill volumes of books so it would be impossible for me to give a definitive account of it here. But essentially, in the first months of the Fine Gael/Labour coalition in 1982, they took a decision to extend 'export credit insurance' to beef products. This insurance was, as the name suggests, to protect Irish suppliers selling into volatile markets such as the Middle East. They decided that this measure would only be extended to two companies, in which Larry Goodman was the main player. Now first off, while many government officials were unhappy with this, it was a wise decision based on the information available to the government at the time. John Bruton stated quite correctly in 1985 that Iraq had the potential to be a very important market for Ireland and that it was an important time for us to open trade with them. No one doubted the governments agenda and indeed no one should. Due to the Iran/Iraq war the export credit insurance was suspended, but the government suggested that it should be reviewed on an ongoing basis and re-instated on the same basis, and to the same companies, at an early opportunity. However the government changed in 1987 and Albert Reynolds was appointed Minister for Industry and Commerce, he duly brought back the export credit insurance for the relevant companies. Two years later Des O'Malley was the minister responsible and he began to raise questions about it and about the level of the insurance. All kinds of allegations were made and O'Malley suggested that 'favouritism' had been shown to Goodman, while Pat Rabbitte said that he had hard evidence that there was major tax evasion and that the revenue commissioners, under political pressure, had turned a blind eye. No evidence was produced to show this so called political corruption over the entire course of the very costly tribunal. What did transpire however was that in some cases EC intervention beef was used for export rather than solely Irish beef, this meant that the government was providing cover for meat that was not even Irish. This was a breach of the rules, however it in no way could be suggested that the Irish government could have known this and the tribunal in its report found that these were specific cases and that there was not a systematic attempt to use EC beef across the board. The government, as far as we on the ground were concerned, was acting in the same good faith as the previous government who instigated the measure. The dispute between Reynolds and O'Malley centered around how much the figure for the insurance actually was, but in truth the real argument was that O'Malley was accusing Reynolds of having acted improperly and shown favouritism to Goodman. Albert was never going to take an accusation like that lying down. When Albert gave evidence at the beef tribunal, he went for O'Malley's jugular. He said O'Malley was 'dishonest'. The barrister questioning him offered him three opportunities to retract the statement but he didn't. 'Dishonest' it was. We expected people to remember what O'Malley had said about Albert, that he had made accusations that were as bad or even worse, but no, suddenly people said Albert was driving them to an election and they didn't want one. The polls bombed. O'Malley, typically indignant, withdrew from government. What a load of arse! My career was tumbling. We were only months running the place and now it was all to be whipped away from me. Well, not if my canvassing could change things! Time to stop playing around at school and get down to serious work.

What an election it was, absolute torture but brilliant at the same time. I suppose we were insulated from the worst of it by being in Longford where Albert was always going to romp home. The national scene wasn't pretty. The electorate felt the election was unnecessary and the media, for its part, started getting stuck into Albert in the most personal and vindictive way. In terms of the media, this election represented a new low. Since then the standard has risen and the personal vitriol is rarely spewed out in the same manner, although it did reach a deplorable low recently in the media's coverage of Liam Lawlor's death.

It was clear from the word go that it was everybody against Fianna Fáil, all lining up for a pop at the title. Fair enough, we were big enough to take them all on, and all at once if they hadn't the guts to come out on their own. It was a tough campaign and at times it seemed that no matter what we said no one was going to listen to us. Albert looked weary and tired, everything got twisted and mangled in the media, and after just a few weeks we were punch drunk already. All the rosaries in the world couldn't pull it out of the fire. We had bombed in the polls but in the end started to show some signs of lifting, and if we had had another week, well, things might have been different.

I remember being in Ballymahon for a meeting after one poll showed us slightly up, and Tony Farrell, the comhairle ceantair secretary, began shaking my hand and telling me they needed more like me. 'Work your way up – and that's what we'll do in this election.' Tony was a great party man, and a gentleman, too; sadly he died of cancer a few years later, still a young man. I was very sad to lose him as a friend and a sponsor in politics. Maybe my career would have been different if he had lived; he certainly would have been a great ally.

We did a strong canvass of our area, combing it as never before. Albert's daughter, Andrea, came with us and she was absolutely fantastic – everyone took her straight to their hearts and she breezed through the canvass, showing no shortage of political ability herself. Of course, you always meet one or two who complained, but bitter auld sods like that are everywhere. One woman who canvassed for independent candidate Tom Fox threw a few jibes about Albert's education (not that she had a great deal more). My father knew best how to deal with those situations. He would just walk away, storing it up for the time being. Years later, when Tom Fox's people came to our door in 1997, he put them in their place. I can still see the gravel rising into the air as they sped away in their cars after the encounter. Don't ever expect to cross Mickey Fallon and get away with it. He was never bested, and you'd want balls of steel to mix it with him.

But in Longford generally the reception we got was fantastic. Even diehard Blueshirts were giving Albert their No. 2 and that was good enough for us. Most people in Longford, whatever their party, knew the worth of the man, and although they might not agree with him, they respected him. Most experienced Party people treated each other well on the doorstep anyway, knowing how tough it was out there.

Andrea had dinner in our house one evening after a day canvassing, and of course my mother pulled out all the stops, the good cutlery and the best china plates were taken out and laid on the table. I got a disapproving look for adding the big plastic container of ketchup, but I never eat anything without ketchup so my mother really should have seen that one coming. Andrea was completely down-to-earth and had no airs or graces at all, which made her very easy to get along with. After dinner we watched the television, and heard the leader of the Labour Party, Dick Spring, say that it would be difficult to work in a government headed by Albert Reynolds. Andrea just threw her eyes up to heaven as my father wrung his hands in protective anger, and I wondered about how tough-skinned a family needs to be when one of theirs is involved in politics. Spring had been persona non grata on our television screen since early November, when he had attacked Albert in a series of vehemently anti-Fianna Fáil speeches. Spring's bitterness made Labour's success at the polls even harder to take.

The night before polling, however, was a night no one in the parishes of Cashel or Lanesboro will ever forget. We in the Fermoyle cumann had our usual end of campaign bash in the Peer Inn, Lisnacusha. In this quiet country area, people went about their everyday work, voted as was their duty, and rarely caused anyone any trouble. But that night a brush with the big time was coming their way, so there was one hell of a bash. There was a huge crowd in the pub; everybody who was anybody in Longford politics made their way there. The gardaí patrolled outside, although they were there for the Taoiseach, not to enforce closing times. The gardaí were decent folk too, who knew that community policing was about working with the people, and every so often the people were going to bend the rules, and you had to let them from time to time in order to keep them on the side of law and order for the rest of the time. A reward for being good folk, you could say. Besides, if we couldn't have a night tonight, when could we have one? If you're a strict moralist, get over yourself, life's too short – just don't harm others and make the most of it.

Albert only arrived in the early hours. Terry Leyden and Mike Finneran and Seán Doherty were already there as his Roscommon running mates. Over in Offaly, Senator Seán Fallon and Minister Brian Cowen were at a function when Fallon turned to Cowen and said, 'It's a pity we aren't in Longford tonight, there's a great pub there and they have a huge party on the last night.' According to the story, Cowen said, 'Ah, sure it will be over now anyway.'

'Not at all,' Fallon told him, 'it will go on all night', so they promptly got in the car and headed off, arriving in the Peer Inn just after Albert showed up. A lot of Roscommon people ventured in, too. Albert's family all came, with people swarming to the ever-popular Andrea. She probably got the biggest cheer of the night when she stood up to sing 'The Cliffs of Doneen'. I asked her if she ever thought about running herself, and she replied, 'No, but the people here might change my mind.'

Government press secretary Seán Duignan was also there, and in his book *One Spin on the Merry-go Round* he gives a very apt summary of the mood that night: 'The speeches were alternately denunciatory, defensive and defiant. The media – the anti-Albert press – were the main targets, with Dublin 4 and PD types close runners-up. There was a mood almost of rural betrayal and abandonment at the hands of the eastern establishment.'

I don't think I could put it better. There was a bitter anger in the air: we felt we didn't get a fair crack of the whip and we were annoyed. For us this night was about getting together and feeling stronger before we faced the next day.

Tea and sandwiches were served in a back room and the night just kept on going. Brian Cowen, crushing my shoulder, telling me not to worry because 'We'll be all right.' Seán Duignan straddling two barstools and my father telling him he got a great job out of it anyway. He clapped me father on the back and said 'Yeah, but I could be unemployed tomorrow.' I shook Albert's hand and promised him we wouldn't let him down. I could have cried when he looked me straight in the eye and said 'Oh, I know you won't.' Seán Fallon putting an arm around me in the doorway of the pub and saying 'By God, the Fallons are out in force tonight.' Terry Leyden drinking tea with me and telling me that I had a winning smile, that I'd be one to watch. Nothing had changed since I was ten really; the later the night got the better I was. The later the night got the more chance we had of winning an overall majority the next day.

But God save us all, polling day was dawning. As the pub cleared you could almost hear the media sharpening their knives. We had staved them off as long as we could; now it was time to abandon the garrison and let the storm break about us. Sometime around 5.30 or 6 a.m. we got into our cars and began heading home.

Polling day followed the usual format but this year everyone's mind was on the national scene. We knew we had the work done in Longford, but the problem lay elsewhere. Exit polls that night did nothing to allay our fears. The day of the count was depressing; people in the count at the mall in Longford were better off not hearing the news from the rest of the country. Fianna Fáil was losing seats all over the shop. Even worse, where we normally were among the first TDs elected, the Party was fighting for later seats this time. Labour were sweeping in at the top of the polls, my father said. He cast the newspapers aside, no longer marking tally figures or seats won and lost, and stared at the television which showed

Labour well ahead in seats won at this early stage.

'We used always be far and away ahead at this time,' he said sadly.

My mother was making tea and cooking, partly to take her mind off things, partly to keep everyone happy, and partly because that's what you do for a funeral. Friends rang and I put a brave face on it, saying we weren't bothered we would go into opposition and rebuild, but the truth was I did feel betrayed. Feck ya anyway, Ireland. We could have done so much, and you threw it in our face. I raged at the cruelty of politics. Struggling to get your message through against the tide, but 'they would not listen, they did not know how, perhaps they'll listen now'. I began to wonder if all you ever try to do is the right thing and still the people inspired by the media kick you in the teeth and accuse you of all sorts, what's the point in being in politics at all? If they don't want to listen, what's the point in even trying? I couldn't begin to describe the level of disillusionment I felt that night going to bed, how utterly futile everything I had done up to that point seemed. This young man's love affair with politics took a bruising. I felt tired and dejected and, at a couple of weeks off sixteen years of age, I felt like I had spent a lifetime in politics and wanted to retire. The Democrats in the States were looking like an attractive prospect, if they wanted me.

But one thing about Irish politics is that you should never expect that what you think is going to happen, will happen. Albert was off in Edinburgh negotiating structural funds for Ireland from the EU. People, including those in the media and some prominent opposition spokespersons, said the Irish team were mad, Maastricht was over-sold and there was no way we would get £6 billion from the EU; the figure would be closer to £4 billion. Oh, yes, that's what they said, they're on record in television interviews and more, although many try to deny it now. Albert walked out of the summit in Edinburgh with £8 billion, the biggest ever injection of cash into the Irish economy. No one could take it from him; he had proven what he could do. In subsequent years Ireland did draw down the full £8 billion, and that's the biggest single reason we had an economic boom in the 1990s. Albert did the business.

And when he did, he changed everything. Suddenly there was a whole new shade appearing for any prospective government, and it was just rosy. Throughout the weeks that followed, Labour vacillated while Fine Gael began imposing strict terms on government. The only option with sufficient numbers to form a government was Fine Gael, PDs, and Labour. But Labour wanted Democratic Left to be brought on board aswell– to keep the balance of left-wing influence on the government, they said. I never believed in that ideological codology, nor did any of our family. When you did something, you asked if it was right or wrong; after that, whether it was left or right didn't matter two shiny shites. They wanted DL in there for the craic, 'twould be great to have the lads in with us', and in truth Labour were already thinking about a left-wing merger.

It all got too much for Spring. Trying to hold the moral high ground, he was surprised by an attack on his flanks which came in the form of an offer from Fianna Fáil to negotiate, with everything on the table, he couldn't say no and be seen as fair, so he met Fianna Fáil. Fine Gael found out and made a blunder; they got all indignant and wouldn't talk any further to Labour until they stopped talking to Fianna Fáil (Montessori teachers will be familiar with this syndrome!). Now Spring knew that if he broke off talks with Fianna Fáil he was at Fine Gael's mercy and would have to take whatever they offered. In the meantime he discovered that even though things like the Taoiseach's job or finance weren't up for negotiation at all, he was still going to get a better bargain from a party he could still walk away from, so he stuck with Fianna Fáil and they made a deal.

Now understand this: we hated Labour at this point. Their behaviour and the things they said during the election were out of order. We had to make a tough decision in our house: either let the other shower in to, as we saw it, 'destroy the economy like they did in the 1980s', or deal with the devil himself, but at least where we would be in control and could keep an eye on Labour's wild ways.

Decision made. Our family and all Fianna Fáilers had a simple rule: Fianna Fáil was good for the country. In fact, Party and country are one and the same thing, therefore the country needs Fianna Fáil at the helm no matter what indignity we had to endure.

Mind you, we wouldn't sell out the country. Labour would quickly find out, as did the PDs, that no leader of Fianna Fáil can afford to be dictated to by the smaller party. 'We are tougher to deal with in government and to get on with, because the membership won't allow principles they believe in to be walked on' – so I was often told in one form or another by various people in the Longford Fianna Fáil machine, and that was good enough for me.

I was playing PE at school when teacher Declan Rowley called me aside to discuss the events. The lads didn't miss me from the game – my lack of height meant I was feck-all addition to a basketball team anyway, unless they sat me up on the hoop itself to catch the ball, which happened on more than one occasion (and it was bloody hard to get down, let me tell you). I explained to him why we needed to get back in government, secretly delighted that Albert was going to be Taoiseach still and that my future career was safe. The principal, Fr Garvey, came over and questioned the merits of going in with the likes of Labour, selling our souls in doing so. To be honest, despite Spring's comments, I didn't mind these Labour boys – power to the people and all that. What was funny was that in the national media the debate was the opposite: how could good upstanding Labour go into government with the devil that was Fianna Fáil?

Ah, the media, they never did understand the Fianna Fáil psyche. It was entirely beyond their comprehension that Fianna Fáil could be a force for good in the world, or even that the vast majority of their readership voted Fianna Fáil. How people mourned the demise of the Irish Press, but in truth in its latter days many Fianna Fáil people didn't buy it as they felt that as a paper it was so obsessed with proving that it was fair that it had as much anti-Fianna Fáil bias as the *Irish Times* or *Irish Independent*. After it went tabloid it got even worse. At many cumann meetings it was often said that the Press would have survived if it hadn't lost its connection with the Party.

Newspapers are a funny thing in a political household. They are studied in detail for every nugget of information, yet reviled and hated for their comment. My father used to deliver the newspapers to Sligo and Ballina, and therefore we always got all three main daily papers (until the *Press* closed and reduced that to two). The *Irish Independent* became more the main staple after the closure of the Press strangely enough; as far as we were concerned it seemed to take on a fairer approach once the competition was out of its way. Certain reporters, like Bruce Arnold, could always make the blood boil, though, as did columnists who appeared from time to time. Columnists were particularly bad. Exonerated from any need to report news, they just made their remarks, and some like Eoghan Harris were particularly infuriating.

I personally had read Fintan O'Toole's column more than once, and even as a teenager I could feel my blood pressure soaring to frightening levels. Anyway, as far as I was concerned, anyone who was so limited in his political perspective, yet continued to try to comment on current affairs, was not worth reading.

The new government confounded its critics, though, and proceeded to work extremely well. Labour got a lot of hassle early on for appointing so many friends and contacts to advisory roles. This was something Fine Gael and Labour always did, and can I say here and now I don't blame them one bit. I see absolutely nothing wrong with a minister wanting to appoint someone they know and trust to a sensitive post. Fianna Fáil, however, has usually tended to appoint advisors and programme managers from the ranks of the civil service, and they have always been excellent in their work. This practice, of course, has never gained Fianna Fáil any credit and in fact I think most people assume we are a party which appoints our friends to jobs, when in fact the opposite is the case. If you want a minister to appoint you to his team, support another party. Then

again maybe I'm just biased because nobody ever appointed me to anything. Feckers.

Jim Stafford, Albert's personal secretary, arranged for me and my mother to tour Leinster House and government buildings. It was a soaking wet day and my poor mother was drenched during the walk from Connolly station to Leinster House. We also had to stop off and buy shoes for me as my mother didn't feel that my trusty Nike Air Jordans were appropriate attire when visiting the Dáil. Jim gave us a personal tour and it was one of the most memorable days I've ever had; it went far beyond the normal tour one would get. But the highlight was getting to sit back in the Taoiseach's chair in his office. Wow, it still gives me shivers. For a couple of minutes I could pretend that all my dreams had suddenly come true.

In the meantime, I was getting in some practice at speaking on my feet as a member of the senior English debating team in St Mel's, something I was very proud of. Mick Lennon, John Devanney and Keith McDonogh were also on the team and we won our regional title in a year when the standard was pretty high. I loved it. This was my sphere. Like all teenagers, I had moments when I felt nervous and awkward at school, difficulty fitting in, but the one thing that was very odd about me was that the only place I felt completely comfortable was when I was in front of an audience speaking. I had no doubts about myself, no fears. I might sometimes wonder when I was sitting in a crowd what people thought about me, but it all disappeared when I stood up to talk. I lived for that moment. The lads at school always turned up in numbers to support us and I loved to watch them smirk confidently as they knew I was going to get up and let fly. We all crave some form of attention and adulation; this was mine. For those few minutes I knew how the lads who played on the football team felt when they walked out onto the pitch.

My fourth year of secondary school would soon be drawing to a close. Unfortunately the recent run of good form with the convent ladies had dried up. Fourth year was a doss and I didn't do enough work at all, though naturally it was only as the year was ending that I began to realise this. Ciarán McGuinness told me he was repeating fourth year, and while I knew it would be the wise thing for me to do, too, I went ahead to the leaving cert year with my friend, Mick, and figured my future was still safe with Albert at the helm.

I knew that the following year at school was to be my last and that I would have the enormous social event that was my graduation ball to contend with. I knew who I was going to ask, and had joined the parish folk group, even though my singing wasn't the best, just so I could get talking to her and spring the question in good time.

That summer we had a school tour to Austria. I packed my best selection of pro-EU teeshirts and got ready to go. The tour was typical of what happens when you let thirty-eight teenage boys loose. We took the boat from Rosslare to Cherbourg, and met up with a girl's school from Limerick along the way. I was lucky enough to hang around with Mick, whose good looks always ensured there were plenty of girls milling about us. Teenagers wherever they go look to mate; they simply can't help it. I met a girl with the won-derfully exotic name, Simone, 'Limerick must be a great place' I thought.

The summer flew by, and come September I was back in school, having a bit of a panic as reality set in that this was my final year and at the end of it was the exam that would have the single biggest influence on my life to date. Bloody marvellous. One teacher, Miss Daly, very kindly informed us that if we hadn't worked up until now we could still make it up if we put our heads down. I took a lot of consolation from that. I could never understand the teachers who told you that if you hadn't done anything last year you were in big trouble now. Eh, excuse me, but it's a bit late. Some encouragement might help, you know!

It was a time of change nationally. The Downing Street declar-ation was set to change the whole mood of events in the north; violence was coming to an end and we weren't even fully aware of it. It was a huge diplomatic achievement by Albert Reynolds. I had grown up in a generation that was immune to stories about murder and bombings in the north. You could sit every night doing your homework, and while you might be distracted by someone being gunned down in Paris, once the news reverted to the cycle of death and violence in the north, you tuned out again and went back to your sums. I had only visited the north on one occasion and even then it felt like we were determined to get out of it as quickly as possible. Longford is only 35 miles from the border and it was a shame that these counties seemed to be cut off from us, not so much by the physical border as by the fear engendered by years of terrorism on all sides. All efforts at peace had come to nothing. John Hume and Seamus Mallon of the SDLP went out on a limb and tried to bring Sinn Féin in from the cold so to speak. They were heavily criticised for this, but they knew it was necessary. Albert Reynolds was a pragmatic business man, he brought that approach to everything, he was nationalist in his outlook, but he abhorred violence. He did not have any of the baggage that many political leaders carry with them, instead he believed that, just as in business, there must be a way to make a deal in any circumstance. He moulded a series of meetings and documents into a peace process. Reynolds never shied away from tough negotiation and in managing to bring about the 'Downing Street declaration', in conjunction with John Major, he had opened up a whole new opportunity for peace. There was now for the first time, a clear statement that the British had no economic interest in the north and the right to self-determination on all sides was recognised. It was this that paved the way for para-militaries to call a ceasefire.

The government seemed to be settling well and I thought at the time that I would have no distractions during this most important of school years. Keith McDonogh had left the debating team and was replaced by Pádraig Loughrey, who normally debated *as Gaeilge* and was a great speaker. We really felt that we could go all the way that year but unfortunately on 6 December we lost to Newtownforbes convent. I have to make the point here and now, and sorry to all Newtownforbes students reading this, but it was a terrible decision – few people at the debate could understand it. Perhaps we blended our refutation too well in our speeches; it was so seamless the judges didn't see it. We were devastated. We should have won that night and could have gone on to take the title.

In recent years I have helped to train debating teams in other schools and adjudicated debates myself, and I have to say that I am often disappointed at the level and ability of those competing. We would have mopped the floor with teams who win All-Irelands now in some debating competitions. And until Ireland applies an oral English exam, it's going to get worse. No one really bothers to cultivate the art of oration in youngsters anymore. Why would they? It's not like they will get any points for it.

In February we had our graduation dance and I brought the lovely Ruth Donnellan as I had planned. She was the perfect date – entertaining, fun and an absolute lady. Tense occasions, grad dances: we were one of the few couples there who didn't end up having a row. For me it was another of those huge social occasions which I felt I navigated successfully, and doing so helped keep up my self-styled imaginings of being the future Taoiseach.

It seemed that the gods were conspiring against my leaving cert, though. My Dad took ill and was diagnosed with diabetes, which meant a stay in hospital. I had always seen him as utterly indestructible, and it was a harsh wake-up call to watch him go into hospital. He had retired a year or so earlier, which was just as well now.

Of course, as a son I could be relied on to make the whole situation worse. I brought the car to school and managed to get smashed into by a lorry – it came across the road, hit the car and then took off. Wonderful. Breaking that news was not something I wanted to do. Dad took it well, though, and his only concern was that I get back driving as soon as possible. I did, a bit nervously to begin with, I must admit.

One of the great events of the year was when we won yet another

Leinster title. Considering that St Mel's population was drawn mostly from Longford, with a few from Westmeath, Roscommon and Leitrim, none of which are dominant counties in terms of the GAA, the school's success in completely controlling Leinster colleges GAA for over seventy years is all the more surprising. By God, were those matches good craic. Getting out of school early to go to the games, singing all the way through, and weekend celebrations of victories – it didn't get much better at seventeen!

I worked hard in my last year, trying to make up for lost time. Hard by my standards anyway, though there were setbacks. Like history. My history teacher was a Labour supporter, God help his poor lost soul, and we didn't exactly get on. I got thrown out, in fact. Fine, I'll study history on my own, I thought, I don't want it coloured by all that Labour propaganda anyway. All in all, the year wasn't really going my way, but I was confident that with a bit of study I could turn it all around, despite the big distraction of Ireland playing in the World Cup.

But May had another surprise in store. We were revising, at this stage, and I was carrying practically all my notes and books in my bag. We got off early on a Wednesday and I left mine along with other schoolbags in the cathedral car park. It sounds stupid but it was what you did rather than lug a heavy bag around. Anyway, who wants to steal a schoolbag? Well, someone bloody did, and they feckin' stole mine! Everything was gone; all my notes, books, the lot. At first I thought someone had hidden the bag for a laugh, but alarm bells began ringing as the time passed. Dad drove in to help me look but the search came to nothing. My mother decided that the only thing to do was to ring the local radio station, Shannonside FM. The fact that my back was stolen was now broadcast across several counties in an area with a huge listenership. Within minutes, the phones were ringing.

'Did ya hear, Johnny Fallon's bag was stolen.'

This material was gold dust for a right good slagging. I was just grateful that there were only a few weeks left in school, but until then I had to grin and bear it. When I went to Miss Daly to explain at the start of class why I had no homework done, she started to tell me, 'Look, if this is an excuse to get out of homework, I really don't want to hear …' She was cut off by Paddy Greene as he ambled towards his desk. 'Oh, no, Miss, that's the truth. It's all over the radio. Didn't you hear?' Thanks, Paddy.

The bag never did show up. I prayed every night that the thief's left leg would wither and develop a wobble, he would be easy to pick out then, but that didn't work either. My mates were good at giving notes and stuff and teachers offered books to help me revise, but the departure of my schoolbag did a lot of damage to my study and I didn't really recover. Mind you, I got a bit of help from Fianna Fáil. They gave away free copies of the Irish language magazine *Mahogany Gaspipe* at the Árd Fheis, and I used the main article in that edition to practice Irish translation. The topic turned up as a question on the higher level Irish paper in the exam, and helped me turn a definite fail into a pass. Thank God for the Party!

Exams are a surreal experience. The weather is usually fine, and generally it's the time of year when you are feeling good about life and school and everything else. As the exams start you realise you're in school, but at the same time you're not. The place is half deserted except for the students doing exams, and you have this image that you somehow look cool and serious, walking around with your books under your arm. You say goodbye to everyone on the last day of school only to see them again in a few days, and then, depending on what exams everyone is doing, you never get to say goodbye properly to some at all. As a student you are never quite sure if you are still under school authority or not, if you can avoid wearing the uniform and maybe slip in wearing a pair of jeans instead. You think that leaving school will be a huge momentous occasion, a day you will remember forever, your whole young life leading to this point. In truth it passes by with barely a whimper. Still, at the last exam, Economics, for the first time in my life I waited until the end, even if I spent the last minutes reliving Ray Houghton's

goal against Italy a few days earlier. God save Ireland! Revenge for
Scillachi at last!

I left the exam hall and walked up the avenue of the school,
pondering my future and wondering if this was really it, all those
years finally over. Could it be that I was no longer a St Mel's student?
School can be a pain in the ass but it is also the last time in your
life when you can live with no responsibility whatsoever, and your
biggest worry is whether St Mel's can win their thirtieth Leinster
title or not.

5

NEW BEGINNINGS, DISASTROUS ENDINGS

The results came out in August. Mam and Dad had gone to Dublin on the train that day, I can't remember why but I know it was pretty important at the time, so I collected my results on my own. I got a total of 300 points and though it was a long way off the pleasant surprise I got in the junior cert, it was better than I had really expected. I was pretty happy, if not exactly elated. Mick was more or less in the same boat and we sat for a while on the stairs in school, laughing about how we had scraped by yet again. I met my parents off the train, and though they weren't over the moon they were happy I passed the subjects and hadn't made a show of myself anyway. So out I went to Jester's nightclub to celebrate, and did it in style. Next morning I headed off to Lahinch with the Civil Defence unit's first aid team.

I was in Clonmel for the fleadh when the CAO sent out the offers of college places. I hadn't given much thought to it when I filled the form, and now I couldn't even remember what I had marked down. I rang home to see what college places I had been offered. I thought I was going to Athlone IT, but apparently social studies had taken a big jump in points and I wasn't going to get that. Instead, my mother and sister told me, I was being offered a place in Dundalk for business studies (management and administration). That was news to me: when did I apply for that?

Not having taken geography as a subject, my next question was 'Where is Dundalk?' The phone was passed to my father, who told me it was past Drogheda and somewhere near the border. That's all I need, I thought, to be shot before I even bloody start.

A few weeks later Mam and Dad brought me up to Dundalk and helped me find digs near the train station; I'd be bringing my bike up and down to college each day. The landlady, Maureen

Martin, seemed friendly enough and the room was comfortable, so I reckoned I was going be all right. I knew just one other person going to Dundalk, Ross Carr, and he was doing engineering, which meant he would have a very different timetable to me.

Even though I tried to convince my mother that I would be fine on my own she was determined that she and Dad would come up for the registration day and settle me into the digs. Luckily, Albert had my best interests at heart and shortly before I went to Dundalk negotiated the ceasefire in the north. That at least calmed my fears of a premature end to my budding political career.

In fact, Albert was really cruising, getting a standing ovation in the Dáil from all sides. I remember watching and saying to my father, 'He is untouchable now. That surely must guarantee another election after this term.' It was hard to see anyone rejecting a man who could claim such political success. Albert had always believed that he could bring all sides in the north around the table. To be honest I don't think anyone believed him. He often said at meetings that it was his aim to get the IRA to lay down its arms, and if they did that loyalist paramilitaries would follow suit. While we supported his endeavours wholeheartedly, even we did not believe he would actually manage to do it. He has often said that at the time he was a 'minority of one'. There is a lot of truth in that, but no one can ever take away the achievement of this goal from him, and it was due to his self-belief and hard business style. He was the right man at the right time and Ireland owes him a debt for that at least.

There were stories floating around about problems and gripes, something to do with the president of the High Court and Fianna Fáil wanting to appoint the attorney general, Harry Whelehan, which Labour didn't. Nothing serious. Nothing to threaten the stability of the government. Even my father, who tended to see problems everywhere, seemed content that all was well for the foreseeable future. We were even gaining a certain respect for Dick Spring, and that was really saying something. The beef tribunal made its report. I think it is important to point out our mood on the ground as this was happening. Despite all the talk of it, we in no way feared the report, our knowledge of Albert convinced us that he would not have done the things he was being accused of. He was a risk taker and a gambler, yes. A good leader has to be. Politicians take tough decisions, sometimes they are wrong, shed-loads of taxpayers money was lost in Irish Shipping and the Dublin Gas Company in the mid eighties because politicians got the decision wrong, but no one was holding a tribunal into that. We also knew that over the course of the tribunal which dragged on for years, not one shred of evidence was produced to link Albert Reynolds to Larry Goodman, or to show he influenced the process unfairly, or that he acted improperly or beyond his remit at any stage. Lets face it we had the age old problem, a few people were standing up making accusations with no proof, but the accusations were more fun than the truth. Not a single person I knew in Fianna Fáil in Longford was in anyway surprised when the tribunal stated quite clearly that there was no evidence whatsoever to suggest that Reynolds had done anything wrong. Of course, if the report had said Reynolds was at fault everyone would have said it was a great report, but instead because the tribunal based its report on evidence and therefore cleared Reynolds name, it was immediately dismissed as 'whitewash' and the old accusations, still without foundation or evidence, were trotted out again. You just have to get used to that with politics.

One of the difficult things about coming from Longford is that you are forced to leave home early. Jobs are limited and there is no college there, so you end up moving out, and that's not easy at seventeen. Mam and Dad did travel up and helped me register and dropped my bag off at the digs, then they caught the train back to Drogheda where they were staying with my aunt. It was a hot autumn day, and I walked them to the railway station. They were both waving and crying as the train pulled out; I watched it till it disappeared around the corner, and then stood for a few moments in the silence, thinking 'Well, Johnny boy, you've really done it this time. You don't know a soul, have never even been here before, and haven't a clue what you are studying. Christ, you should have worked at school.' It began to dawn on me that I would only be seeing my home at weekends from now on, and I didn't like that feeling one iota. 'When I left my home and family, I was no more than a boy, in the company of strangers, in the quiet of a railway station, running scared.' For the first time in my life my confidence deserted me, and when I got back to my empty room I really began to doubt myself.

But, if I have ever been anything in my life it's irrepressible. I just won't allow myself to get depressed for very long. Besides, there were girls at college. Girls? They were women! And although unnerving after five years of all-male education, I was more than up for the challenge. Soon enough, I settled into the swing of things in college, and I went home at weekends, where the fire would be roaring, my father bursting to tell me all the news, chatting about politics and football, my mother with a big feed ready and one of her world-famous apple tarts sitting on the table. This was living.

But winter was approaching and with it, as always, came political disaster. November 1994 changed my life completely; I often sit and wonder where I would be now if it had all been different. Disaster never hit us as hard as it did that month. My political fortunes were dealt a final blow as everything I had believed in came crashing down.

It was all about Harry Whelehan ostensibly, although let me tell you here and now that Harry is a gentleman, one whose only crime was that he was just too good. When Harry made a call as attorney general and it went to the courts, he was proven right. He did his job, and a finer legal mind you could not find. Labour refused to say, and to this day have never clarified, what exactly their problem with Whelehan was. Their argument that he was too conservative is laughable. The law is either there or not, and it's not up to the judge to make it up; he only applies the laws we as a state make. Conservative or radical, he cannot influence that law.

The news dragged on about the case of Fr Smyth, and an extradition file that had not been dealt with. The media were chasing up outrageous stories of a cover-up where none existed. The thing was it was all in the past, and Smyth had since been arrested and prosecuted, but questions remained over the delay in answering a request for his extradition. Whelehan told cabinet that the delay happened because the legislation in question had not been applied before, namely the fact that the crimes were committed so many years before the request, and they needed to be sure that the extradition legislation would cover it.

Whelehan gave his explanation to cabinet on the day that they were due to vote on his appointment as president of the High Court. Labour walked out of the cabinet meeting when discussions of the appointment began. We were astounded. Could it be that this petty thing was going to blow up? Then we heard they only absented themselves to distance themselves from the appointment of Whelehan as president of the High Court, which was made by the remaining ministers at the cabinet meeting once Whelehan had explained what happened with the Brendan Smyth file. Still others talked of a cover-up, and spread rumours that Cardinal Daly, Whelehan and Reynolds were conspiring. I mean, who writes this crap? Did editors really need to go to college and study journalism if this was what passed as reporting? It is crucial to note that two by-elections had been held during the previous week and Fianna Fáil had lost both. As a result, there was a subtle change in the Dail arithmetic. Fianna Gael, Labour and Democratic Left could now form a coalition that was not possible after the 1992 general election.

Albert made a spirited defence of Whelehan in the Dáil the following week. I stayed home from college and listened to it on the radio. A new Attorney General, Eoghan Fitzsimons, was appointed – thrown in at the deep end, might be a better way of saying it. Nothing could have prepared him for what was to follow, starting a new job in the middle of one of the worst crises in decades. He was asked to carry out an investigation over a matter of hours, and in that time he had to familiarise himself with new cases, new personnel and differing legal opinions. Most difficult of all, he had to try to adjust to how politicians worked. One can see from the evidence given before a Dail committee set up to investigate the matter, that it is debateable to this day whether Fitzsimons or Whelehan were correct in their reading of events. But when other cases were discovered Whelehan was happy at first, as they proved he never covered up this type of case and always speedily dealt with it. The political mood, however, had changed.

The issue was no longer about the law or the application of our laws. It was plain politics now. Whelehan's or Reynold's good names were irrelevant, it was about getting heads. Democratic Left front bench spokesperson Pat Rabbitte was standing up as usual in the Dáil, saying all sorts of things under privilege. This time he said, 'There is a document that will rock the foundations of this society to it's very roots.' Good man, Pat. If someone had a headache, Pat would make it a brain haemorrhage. In fact he would probably make it a brain haemorrhage epidemic. This was one stupid comment too many and ensured his entry in our family blacklist, from which there is no return. He is included in various prayers that we offer up for the sake of the nation. Nothing bad, just a prayer that God will make people on the list look foolish; and, thankfully, God has seen fit to grant such requests from time to time.

Ireland were playing Northern Ireland that week and the team was training in Oriel Park in Dundalk. Myself, Keith Farrell, David Hanratty and a few other Drogheda and Dundalk lads decided to hop the wall and watch them. We went in at the very back of the stand and stayed well quiet, but it only lasted a few minutes before Jack Charlton threw a hissy fit and demanded we be removed. For feck's sake! Big Jack could be a contrary auld shite at times. I wouldn't mind, but one of the lads was a season-ticket holder at Oriel Park, and was getting thrown out of his own ground. No one appreciates the League of Ireland or its fans enough, certainly Jack didn't. We couldn't climb back over the wall – we had a bloody big drop getting in – we had to cross the pitch instead. Roy Keane winked at us as he sprinted by, which was great because although he was a hero I thought for a minute he might break my spindly legs for the craic. Goalkeeper Packie Bonner looked up and said, 'Are they kickin' ye out, lads? Don't worry, we'll make up for it tomorrow.'

I rang home the following day, and they didn't seem confident that the government could be saved. What a disaster. Were we to face an election after all? By 10.30 that morning I got a call to tell me there was a rumour that all had been settled and an agreement reached. By midday I heard that Labour reneged on the deal and it was all over; the only way to save the government would be for Albert to resign. Albert proceeded to give the speech which had originally been meant to patch things up, condemning Whelehan and saying he was wrong. Albert regretted that speech later, when it was proven that this was not the case.

It later turned out that Spring had agreed to save the government on the basis that Albert had not known about other legally similar cases when he made his speech defending Whelehan on the Tuesday. However, an hour or so after agreeing to stay in government he contacted Eoghan Fitzsimons and asked him when he had told the Taoiseach about the other cases. He also reminded Fitzsimons, strangely enough, that he was not under any obligation to answer the question. I always thought that strange, maybe he didn't want to hear the answer, in any event Fitzsimons informed Spring that he had told Reynolds about his view of other cases, before the Monday speech. According to Fitzsimons Spring simply replied 'oh lord Eoghan, we will both end up back at the law library'. Spring withdrew from government on the basis of what Fitzsimons had said.

To be fair reading back over evidence later on, Fitzsimons did believe that he had told everyone the details on Monday morning. However, he was not experienced in dealing with politicians and never made the situation clear, he didn't seem to realise that politicians could only act on hard evidence and could not accept his advice until he put it in writing and was fully sure. It is also clear that the civil servants in the Attorney General's office who had the most experience in these cases disagreed with Fitzsimons view. Mr Russell who was the senior official dealing with extradition cases in the attorney general's office took most of the blame. It is important to point out that the Attorney General's office at the time was greatly under resourced and not even computerised. Overburdened officials often had to make judgement calls and try to deal with the most serious cases first. As there was a question mark over the validity of the request and as Fr Smyth was believed to be under the surveillance of the Church authorities, the file was not considered a priority. You have to remember that this was a time when Ireland still trusted the Church in the main, this was long before the Ferns report and there was no reason for anyone to believe that Church authorities would hide, move or protect a paedophile. Mr Russell would appear to have been right in his assumption that the legislation had not been tested before, but wrong in his administrative prioritisation of the case. It is worth letting people know that he was one of the finest legal minds in the country, the recognised expert on extradition and his academic achievements included being one of the youngest ever Reid professors of law at Trinity College. If he disagreed with Fitzsimons view then that disagreement had to be taken seriously. One can only imagine the confusion this must have caused in government circles. Spring later used this as a reason not to go into government with Fianna Fáil under Bertie Ahern and instead formed the rainbow coalition. Looking back now, the government seemed to fall for no good reason. The excuses given at the time later fell through, and we can now see that there had, in fact, been no wrongdoing by any member of the government. If only calmer heads had prevailed!

I went down to MJ's pub to watch the match that night. Ireland won 4-1, but I couldn't even enjoy it. After the match, I got up to go and a girl in the class, who was really stunning, stopped me and held my hand. 'Ah, don't go. Sure stay and celebrate the match,' she said. I looked at her and simply replied, 'Albert is gone, I've nothing to celebrate,' and turned away. She was quite rightly peeved at my snubbing her invitation for such a stupid reason as politics. I made the long walk back to my digs feeling utterly depressed, confused and miserable.

It's funny how, when you follow politics, your life becomes totally entwined with an individual politician. He or she becomes like your patron, and your success often depends on the progress of their career. I sat in the digs watching Albert's resignation speech through my tears, and truly wished that I was many years older like the other people I knew in politics and could say, 'We've had our day, it's up to someone else now' and happily retire. But I was too young for that. I suddenly began to realise that making my way in the world was going to be a lot more difficult than I'd really thought. I rang the Reynolds household to express my support and best wishes. What else could I do? I took some consolation from Albert's words: 'the highs outweighed the lows'.

It has often been said that, during the years in opposition that followed, Fianna Fáil was like a punch-drunk giant, not knowing what hit it. If that was the case nationally, it was even more so in the organisation in Longford. To go from being the leading lights of the Taoiseach's constituency right down to zero was a terrible blow. We didn't even talk politics at home for a couple of weeks; it was like we all wanted to walk away, like a kind of death that we didn't want to mention. Meetings were held as normal but they all just ended up trying to find reasons for what had happened. However, when Spring went on to reject Bertie Ahern and Fianna Fáil in order to form a rainbow coalition, it stung something deeper in all of us, especially my father. He immediately sprang into action, lashing out at Labour and the new rainbow at every opportunity.

It was a difficult time for us politically as we tried to adjust to being in opposition, something Fianna Fáil are never that comfortable with. The feeling that the country and its finances were our responsibility could not be removed from our veins. I loved to taunt the Blueshirts by reminding them that the people didn't elect this government, it only came into being by default. I nearly got a smack for saying it – but, then, I couldn't blame them for being angry, 1982 was the last year that the people speaking with one voice returned them to power. That's a long wait.

With all that was happening politically it was hard to find time to study at college. Let's be fair, my priority was always going to be looking after my political interests and, after that, ensuring I had some form of social life. It was also about this time that I got into the habit of drinking Guinness. I was always a very thin guy and people told me that if I drank a pint of Guinness every night I'd put on weight in no time. I took to it with a vengeance. Needless to say, after a couple of months I was a lot closer to becoming an alcoholic than putting on a single ounce of weight. I lived on McDonalds and Guinness, but they had no impact on my weight. Supersize me, me arse.

I got the head down and managed to get fairly decent results in my first semester, but we were still covering a lot of old ground that I knew from the leaving certificate. The second semester was more difficult but I managed to scrape by, having not done a whole lot of study. Thankfully, I had a great ability to retain most of the information from what few lectures I was at and this compensated for my aversion to study.

When the summer break came it was a great chance to simply enjoy being at home in Longford again with my family. I worked on a student summer work scheme, pulling up weeds and mowing lawns at a local enterprise centre. I also spent a lot of the summer, which is the political silly season, trying to resurrect my love life, which had a decidedly on and off cycle to it over the course of the previous year. My best efforts there had all failed.

During my second year in college I was more settled. I moved into a house in Mary Street South, a tiny two-bedroomed terrace house, and into this we fitted seven girls and three fellas. It was pretty squashed, but it made for cheap rent. We had wild parties night after night, and more than a few neighbours who weren't one bit impressed.

In second year I met Rory O'Connor and Pamela Sharkey, and between us we embarked on setting up a Fianna Fáil unit in the college, the Brian Lenihan cumann. Brian had died that year and it was apt that the cumann be named after him. We were up and down to Dermot Ahern's office in Francis Street looking for assistance in getting the whole thing off the ground. Dermot, who was Fianna Fáil chief whip at the time, was a tremendous help. He came to meetings and offered any help we wanted, and his secretary, Christine Maguire, was also more than helpful, as well as being great craic. I began to pop down to the office just to sit and chat.

Knowing of the problems Ógra can cause and the mistrust of their voting power by the senior organisation, I set out to convince Party members that this cumann would be properly run. I got a list of cumann secretaries and set out on my bike. Some of them were well outside the town but I made the trip to anyone I could so as to introduce myself and let them know what we were about. I think it paid dividends, because for the rest of the year we got nothing but support from the senior party. And it was right down my alley, sitting in people's living-rooms drinking tea and eating platefuls of scones and sandwiches like the starving student I was, and talking politics all night. I got on much better with older people than younger ones.

Dermot Ahern involved us in everything, and we were invited to any event going. I was asked to speak on The Week in Politics to give a view on the northern Ireland peace process. The IRA ceasefire had collapsed and things weren't going so well. Nick Coffey was the interviewer and there was a small panel comprising myself, Rosemary Farrell, Derek Watters, Noel Lennon and Pearse O'Hanrahan, all of whom were part of Louth CDC, and Nick met us in Dermot's office for the interview. I had been practising what I wanted to say in my dreams the night before, and was thrilled to have such an opportunity. Once the interview moved in my direction I let fly and gave it my all. Thankfully, it came across well on the television, and was replayed over and over at home. Mam and Dad were thrilled. I was especially pleased when Dermot said that he was impressed. Nick Coffey remained a very good friend of mine after that and always reminds me that he expects big things from me. Well, I don't know if I lived up to that billing, but I certainly enjoyed it and all the attention at the time.

Unfortunately, life at college was often a bit too good. The craic with all the gang in the house was brilliant. Ger, Wiggie, Jenni Heylin, Jennii Healy, Irene, Georgina, Kathleen, Kelly, Niamh and Emma were like family, which I suppose we had to be when we all had to squash into one room in a house where we could hardly afford the oil for heating! Wiggie dragged a bag of coal all across the town one night after he had a few pints. I don't know where he got it and didn't want to know either; all that mattered was it would provided much-needed warmth in the depths of winter. It is always hard to keep in touch with people you get to know at college – distance and career often makes it impossible – but there is no doubt you definitely make some great friendships there. Sadly, all things end; Emma was tragically killed in a motorcycle accident a few years later, it shocked us all deeply.

Second year had a couple of tough subjects, like costing. All my life I hated maths and ever since I started secondary school I despised accountancy, so to be fair I knew I was royally screwed the day they told me I'd be doing costing, which was a cross between maths and accountancy! And people actually mange to say this as if the damn subject is going to be remotely interesting.

I sat the exams and had been happy overall, but unfortunately when the results arrived I had to repeat costing. This meant that I wouldn't be allowed to return directly to college to pursue the diploma. Once I passed the repeat and got my national certificate I could take a year out and then go back, if I hadn't found a career by then. It really bugged me after that when people would try to dismiss RTC qualifications; the rules in fact make graduating every bit as hard as in universities. Some years later the RTCs were upgraded to Institute of Technology status, which has helped students in some ways to compete with the university heads.

The other big problem was that throughout the year the costing lecture had been first thing in the morning and I rarely if ever managed to roll out of the bed in time, so I had no notes either to help me study through the summer. I decided to call up the best student in the year, Linda Keenan, who told me to come to Dundalk and she would give me all her notes. It was the best news I got all summer. However, it was a typical Irish summer's day when I went to Dundalk, and I was soaked to the skin by the time I met Linda in the Imperial Hotel where she worked. She didn't have the damn notes with her, so she told me to walk to her house and her sister would give them to me. I got another soaking on the way and then stood outside ringing the doorbell until I finally gave up, emptied the water from my shoes, wrung out my jacket and headed back into town in the lashing rain. Feckin' hell, couldn't God give me one decent break here! Linda was furious when I arrived back in the hotel, saying her sister should have been there, and she apologised profusely to me and promised she would post the notes on. To be honest I thought that was the last I would ever hear; it would cost a fortune to post them and why should Linda even remember? I got back on the train home, puddles forming beneath my feet. My underpants were stuck to me and I was already sneezing. Perhaps my luck had finally run out.

To make matters worse, I was on the dole, which wasn't the most pleasant experience. I hated saying to people that I didn't have a job. When I arrived back in Longford, I went into Longford garda station to get the dole slip signed. My local station was Newtowncashel but the hours that the station was manned were irregular so it was easier to go into Longford town. Normally there was no problem, but on that day when I went in a big lummox of a garda was behind the counter and refused to sign the slip. 'You have to go to your local station, sure I don't know ya.'

'Look!' I said, 'my local station hasn't got a garda yet and it's rarely manned, and the guards who do man it don't know me any better than you. But the point is, God knows when they will be there, and I wasn't around today to find out the time and go up'

The garda looked at me sternly. 'Didn't have time now, is it? Listen here, young fella, you're supposed to be available for work. Are you telling me you weren't around, now?'

Ah, now come on, I mean how bright was this spoon? 'I was trying to sort out revision for repeats at college, so I can get off the dole,' I told him.

'College? Sure you shouldn't be on the dole then.'

Oh, Jesus give me patience. In the end, out of sheer frustration, I told him he could stick the whole damn lot up his hairy arse for all I cared, if he was that thick.

A few days later Linda sent the notes in the post and I sat the exam, and had no difficulty passing this time around. I consoled myself with the thought that at least I had my certificate now, that at least had to count for something. My Dad heard that there was a job going in CIE in Longford, office admin work, and he told me to go for the interview. I didn't need to be asked twice. CIE Longford was a second home to me after all the years that Dad had spent working in it.

I turned up to meet Cyril Hussey, who was a good friend of my father's, and the other interviewer was the station master. Apparently, I almost had the job but they eventually settled on the final person that they interviewed. Cyril Hussey later told both me and my Mam that he felt sorry for me saying, 'It would have been a start for you at least.' He knew how much I liked the old CIE station in Longford. He was right, it would have been nice. I have often wondered how different my life would have been if I had got the job. I am quite sure I would have remained in Longford, perhaps run for council, and certainly would have a lot less money now. But that's life; you never know how the slightest thing is going to change everything forever.

6
JOBS FOR THE BOYS

I went back to Dundalk for one day to celebrate my graduation. Lillian Dowd, who was a very good friend and whose family were good Fianna Fáil stock, came with me. It was a great day, made all the more memorable for me by the fact that many of the board of the VEC were connected with Fianna Fáil and were on the podium, and when I received my certificate they stood up and shook hands, each one calling me by name. I was very proud, not of my educational achievement, but of the feeling that I really had a positive impact on political life in Dundalk.

Months rolled by on the dole and nothing seemed to be happening for me. I certainly felt that, if there was one way to end a political career, it was by ending up on the dole, unless of course you decided to run for Sinn Féin. I hated it, meeting the lads at the weekends for a few pints, heading into Blazers, chatting up a few women until they asked you what you do.

'I'm on the dole.'

'Oh, good for you,' they might say, but you could tell how embarrassed they were at having asked, and how they couldn't hide wondering if you were just a waster. Yeah, I had a few laughs, but it was depressing and demoralising. To make matters worse, far worse, my Dad suffered a heart attack. None of us could believe it. It was always a joke that because he got so wound up he was a prime candidate for it, but it was no laughing matter now.

I applied for a job in a new commercial bank that was opening in Dublin. I thought that I was in luck. It was an entry level position and I had more than just the basic requirements, but the ad also said that they had big expansion plans so it was a good time to get involved and they were eager to get staff together and get things moving. So I got my CV together and I was soon called for an aptitude test. This was a straightforward test and I was told that I scored well in it, so I figured that things must be going all right. I was called to an interview, and then I was called to a second interview where they even took my photograph. But as the weeks passed by I was getting a bit pissed off: how many times were these guys going to call me back before making up their minds?

Me, Mam and Dad attended Fianna Fáil's seventieth anniversary dinner, and every politician was lobbied on my behalf, especially Albert. But to be fair to them, none of them really had any contact with commercial banks outside of Ireland and there wasn't a whole lot they could do.

Finally the call came to ask me to attend for final interview. I was elated; at least this time I knew it was the last hurdle. Mam and Dad travelled up for the day as moral support. But to say it was a disaster would be an understatement. I don't know what the bank thought they were trying to do, but the whole set-up was plainly ridiculous. I felt like I was the butt of a bad joke. There was a large group of applicants there, and we were told we would be there for the day. It started with myself and three others being ushered into a room, with a stern-looking individual assigned to each of us, and we were then told to come up with a marketing plan!

OK, I had learned all about this at college. In fact, I had also learned that it was generally considered flawed and inaccurate, especially in the Irish situation. But they were looking to identify leaders, facilitators, followers and so on. They could label you, stamp you, and stick you in a pigeon hole. Try to remember that this is all for a bloody telephone job, with a salary of less than £10,000 per annum. We are not talking high-fliers; we were being recruited to the bottom of the food chain. Anyway, although politics prepares you for much it can also hamper you; this scenario didn't suit me at all, and the whole time I wanted to turn around and explain to those observing us how they were getting this process all arseways. In general I liked Americans, but I was beginning to understand why some people did not.

The day didn't get any better and if they were trying to stress me out and piss me off it worked. There were three separate interviews, and I found the tone of each progressively more condescending and insulting. 'You got a B in pass math in the leaving cert?' in that slow American drawl.

'Eh, yes, that's correct'

'Don't you think that's poor? Were you just not up to honours standard?'

I bluffed and gave the standard answer about time and interests etc like the books recommend, but I really wanted to tell him just how much tougher our maths exams were than anything in the States, and for his information if I had done honours maths and got an A I wouldn't be sitting here looking for his piss-arse job. Perhaps I should have said that, because every question was a put down. Why did I only get a cert, not a degree, in college? Did I find Irish politics a neat little pastime and had I ever thought of looking at 'real' politics?

'What's the toughest thing you've ever done for money?' another guy asked me. Being very brassed off at this stage, I was tempted for a fleeting second to reply, 'Sleep with your sister,' but instead I opted for 'I footed turf on the bog.' I got a great laugh at the blank expression that drew. This guy had obviously never even heard of the bog.

'And you guys burn this stuff?'

'Yeah. We also sell bog oak as ornaments to American tourists.'

Another guy, standing looking out the window at the Liffey, turned around and said, 'Gee, the river sure is polluted. You guys should do something about that.'

'Yeah, I'd imagine it's nearly as bad as the east river in New York,' I remarked. He looked around and said, "Touché,' but I think he'd discovered all he needed to know about my cheeky nature and I'm sure his mind was already made up.

Finally, I was led to a room with a phone and a table of documents. 'The phone is going to ring; wait for the call,' I was told.

Jesus, who are these guys? It rang all right. It was a guy claiming to have a shipload of bananas outside the Panama Canal and his money wasn't there to pay the bill. What was I going to do about it?

I bluffed as I searched through the documents. To be quite honest, I wanted to say 'Fuck you and your bananas,' but I gave the spiel on the sheet of paper and promised to look into it and get back to him. The phone rang again after this; would you believe it the same guy? This time with a dying man in Frankfurt who needed an air ambulance to bring him to Dublin, or else he would die. Oh sure, them Germans would know nothing about healthcare; better get him back to Dublin and he can go on a waiting list, you spanner. The sheet told me the deadline was passed and no money could be sent, so I told him and he threatened to sue me. Ah, for the love of arse, will you guys get real?

I hardly need to tell you that I didn't get the job. I often wondered if the girl in the very short pink skirt and tattoo just visible on the inside of her right thigh did. As for me, I was totally demoralised. It was my first experience of being interviewed by a really big company, and I was convinced that if that was the norm I was never going to get a job. Being involved in politics had built up an air of confidence in me, a belief in my own ability, but the interview experience hurt me, derided me and made me feel like a complete failure. Thank you very bloody much.

I still scanned the papers, looking for work. My mother chased Albert Reynolds around a function in Ballymahon asking if there was anything he could do for me. 'If I was still there maybe I could, but right now I can't create something. I know how good he is, but...' And he held up his hands. Goddammit, did no one out there appreciate what a terrible impact this implosion in politics was having on my life?

Finally one Thursday I found an advert from Ulster Bank looking for staff. I wasn't too sure after my last experience with a bank, but Dad was, 'Oh, bloody hell, if they can't do something for you

after all our business we gave them. Our mortgage, our account
- sure we've been banking with them for years.' I didn't think that
Ulster Bank were really going to be held to ransom by us; after all,
all we ever had was Dad's CIE wages, and we weren't exactly going
to be appearing on their richest client list! But it was worth a try.

The political lobby swung into action. I don't know if any of
our political contacts really did know anybody in Ulster Bank but
they all said that they would try their best. I never did find out if
anybody had been in contact, but I didn't meet anyone who ever
said it to me in the bank anyway. But what was clear from the off
was that this was an Irish organisation and their approach was far
more practical. I was brought up for the aptitude test and everyone
was told straight off that there would be an interview for successful
candidates and then one final interview after that. I made it through
the first two stages and was called for the final one. It made me
nervous, thinking about what they might have in store, but the staff
in Ulster Bank, Longford, brought me in and showed me around
and told me not to worry, that there would be none of that all-
day test nonsense with them. Armed with my new knowledge of
branch banking, I was ready for the challenge.

I think I also realised the one thing I was possibly doing wrong
in interviews. I cared too much and tried too hard. Yes, you do want
to impress, but you damage your own confidence and composure by
trying to be too much of what you think they want. Dad reckoned we
would get the bus up on the day of the interview. With hindsight, I
think it was the right idea. Without realising it, it gave me a chance
to think, about who I was and where I came from, and if some
banking high-flier scoffed at that, then it was their loss.

The bus wouldn't start at the station in Longford. It was December, just before my birthday in fact, and the frost was having a bad
effect on the engine. We were delayed for nearly forty-five minutes
before ever starting. But hanging around with Dad in the station
reminded me of all the times I had spent there, Dad laughing and
joking with old workmates. We sat beside each other and talked

politics the whole way to Dublin, and how this rainbow coalition was a disaster. The budget increase for pensioners was pathetic, not even the price of a pint, and these guys claimed to be left wing! Yet another reason to believe that all ideologies were bollox. By the time we got to the city centre we were well late, and we raced down the quays, Dad telling me to go on ahead, 'Leave me behind, I can't keep up!' Like I was going to do that; Ulster Bank could wait.

When we got to Georges Quay there didn't seem to be much hurry on them anyway, and they were not in the least put out by my late arrival. After only a few minutes of a wait, I was brought in for interview with Corla Mansfield, then head of recruitment for the bank. She really asked only one question: 'So, tell me a bit about yourself.' That produced a fifteen minute answer that took her right from my schooling to my visit to Ulster Bank, Longford, the week before. It covered my interests and achievements on the way, and when I finished she just said, 'Well, I think that answered pretty much everything I was going to ask. Normally people don't know what to say when I ask that, but you obviously have no problems communicating.' I laughed, hoping that she wasn't going to think I talked too much, which I do tend to do.

'Usually,' she went on, 'I'd ask someone about current affairs, but judging by your references (Albert Reynolds and Dermot Ahern) I know pretty much the answer I'd get, so I suppose you can just tell me what you know of the euro.'

No need to ask me twice. I was on fire now, and took her right through to the finer political points facing the participating countries in the run up to monetary union and why it was the right decision for Ireland. And that, as they say, was that. She winked, shook my hand, and said, 'Don't worry, you'll hear from us shortly.'

I walked out and met with Dad, who was too nervous to even ask how I got on, he just kept talking about this place off Moore Street where we could get an all-day breakfast. He talked about it all the way up to Moore Street. Finally, when we sat down, he asked me, 'Well, how do you think it went?'

I cut up the rasher on my plate, stuffed it in my gob and said, 'Well, Da, if I don't get a job out of that interview, I'll never get one, that's all I know, because I was bloody good in there today.' To say his face lit up would be an understatement. He made me take him step by step through everything I said.

Early next morning I was still in bed and Dad was getting turf at the end of the garden to light the fire. It was a Friday, and the phone was ringing, so I jumped up and answered it. It was the bank. Could I come up to Dublin Sunday night to start work and an induction course on Monday? They would put me up in the Maples Hotel, Glasnevin, until I was settled. I ran out to the back yard where Dad was heeling the turf in the wheelbarrow and told him the news. He nearly cried, and although we were not accustomed to such gestures we hugged each other. Then we got a grip on our emotions and calmed down. Dad went off to take up his favourite hobby: the phone. Everyone had to be rung and told the news straight away, just in case the meaning of this universe-altering event should be lost on anyone.

I felt great, it was coming up to my birthday and I had a proper job. Yes, Johnny Fallon was back, well and truly back.

Of course, word travels fast in rural Ireland, and in no time it was 'Young Fallon got a big job in the bank. Don't you know Albert Reynolds got him into that; it's all who you know.' If only it were true, but I did nothing to dispel such rumours for two reasons: number one, I didn't mind people thinking I had a big job; and number two, what's the harm in annoying a few Blueshirts by letting them think Albert had pulled another stroke? It might even encourage a few more people to join! If only they knew; far from the world of high finance, my early duties in the bank were more concerned with folding statements and cleaning Sunday night's curry chips out of the ATM that some smart-arse thought was funny to stuff in there. Great sport.

I was posted to Edenderry the day before Christmas Eve, and I

settled in quick as there was a great bunch of people in the branch at the time. I was quickly having great political discussions with fellow employees, Hugh Daly and Dave Crowe. I had a damn nice room above Foy's pub for £25 a week. My only problem was that there was a band on beneath me almost every night and they would lift you out of the bed once the vibrations of the drums and bass started, so there was no point trying to sleep, you might as well go down and drink. That was like being a minor celebrity, too. 'Look, there's the new fella in the bank'.

Yes I liked Edenderry, although it wasn't difficult to see that one could take to heavy drinking very easily there, but it wasn't to last. Human resources called the branch.

HQ rarely realises the situation that branches are in. Here they are miles from the top people, a little outpost updated with circulars and the odd phone-call. The employees in a branch are part of the community, and customers expect them to know everything about the bank, but very often they are informed of little beyond their own branch walls. So when human resources rings and you transfer the call to the manager, you spin around and tell everyone because it means only two things: number one, someone or something is about to be done in the branch or has come to the attention of head office. Or number two, someone is about to be transferred. I was sitting at what we called the S40, an enormous old machine into which all dockets had to be keyed, when the manager poked his head around the door. 'Can I have a word with you,' he said. He must have seen the blood drain from my face because when I went into the office he started with, 'Well, the good news is you're not being sacked or anything like that.' Phew! 'You are being transferred to Dublin.'

Shite. A fate worse than death. No one wanted to go to Dublin, with its high costs, while you had the same pay, and become nothing more than another number in the big city. Worse still, you might never get out. I was going to take up a position in the trust company of the bank. I put on a smile but I wasn't happy. I liked the small town atmosphere, and I had only just really started to get settled. And I never liked Dublin. The manager sensed this.

'Look, it would be worse for you,' he said, 'if you were years here and had a bird and everything. This way you can go, no ties. And let me tell you, it won't be the last move you will ever make either.'

Hugh, Dave and myself had been in the basement the previous evenings cleaning out old papers for destruction, a horrible, dusty job, and the next day I looked at Hugh and said to him, 'You can feck off, I'm leaving, so you are not getting me in that basement again.' It wasn't easy to go and leave my new friends behind, though. I got a card, a cake, a pen, a bloody good piss-up and a sore head. Goodbye Edenderry. Despite the endless promises of regular visits to catch up, I never did get to go back, and soon most of the people I knew had been transferred themselves.

7

ABOVE IN DUBLIN

Back to the Maples for three weeks of steak dinners. The bank tried to encourage me to go to a cheaper B&B but I was having none of it; they transferred me so they could foot the bill. After two weeks they insisted I sort myself out, but I still scrounged another week out of them. In the end I took digs with the woman who worked in reception, Pauline, and very comfortable digs they were too. I took up residence on the basis that it was until I found something else, and ended up staying for three years.

Ulster Bank Dublin Trust Company was a very small unit, comprised mostly of women, except for the manager, Finbar Daly. He was a great auld sport, always encouraging and good for a laugh, too. On many evenings I sat after work just chatting away to him about politics or football or whatever happened to take our fancy. Once again, I settled in very quickly, and with an election looming in June it didn't take long before everyone found out my politics.

I think it was also during this time that I discovered part of the reason behind Charlie Haughey's success. I used to go home every weekend, and one Sunday the papers revealed that a former Fianna Fáil minister had received one million pounds from businessman Ben Dunne. My father took one look at the headline and said, 'That's feckin' Charlie.'

'Sure, it could be one of several,' I said, but my father was adamant.

'No bloody way, that's no one else. It has to be Charlie once the figure is around a million. Only Charlie could have the neck to be messing around with a figure like that.' Of course the wily old campaigner was right. Others might be as wealthy, but only Charlie would risk something for those kind of bucks. And Charlie was the only one who continually had question marks over his finances.

We were disgusted, and so was everyone we talked to in the Party. Every member felt let down, so completely betrayed. How could a man who had done so much in the service of the country, and in truth done a good job, have been so foolish, grubby and dishonest in his own finances. What was worse was that the real people Charlie hurt, the ones who were really hit by what he did, were the Fianna Fáil members who travelled to the Árd Fheis every year, those who contributed what they could to alleviate the Party debt, those who slaved year in year out buying and selling raffle and dinner-dance tickets, when all along the Charlie was off buying Charvet shirts with it.

You can picture the distaste we held Charlie in at that time, combined with the fact that he had been ruthless in his dealings with Albert and the rump of his old guard had always been a thorn in our sides. After about a week of speculation the media finally said officially that it was Haughey who had received the money from Ben Dunne. When I went into work the following Monday morning, Trudy, who worked with me and hated Fianna Fáil, marched over, smirking, as I put the kettle on to make tea. 'So now what have you to say? What do you think of Charlie now?' There was no doubt that I had no time for him but I turned smiled and said, 'Ah, Charlie, he was some boyo!' I knew it would infuriate her, and there in part was the secret of Charlie's success: I really believe now that Fianna Fáil rallied so long behind Charlie simply because everybody else was so much against him. If they had all left him alone then it might have allowed Fianna Fáil time to raise questions earlier.

It was a strange time during those months. Fine Gael had been rocked by the Lowry scandal, and it was almost funny watching them grapple with this type of problem, which they had generally lambasted Fianna Fáil for in the past. Lowry was a tough, street-fighting type of politician, and in truth was a big loss to Fine Gael. I have no doubt that had he not become embroiled in shady deals he would have been Party leader one day. But as an opponent you had to take a certain delight in watching their leader, John Bruton, shaking Lowry's hand as he resigned and saying, 'My friend, my best friend forever.' My Dad, happy in the knowledge that the damage was done, sat back and for once felt no need to shout, instead muttering just one word to sum up the situation. 'Bollocks.'

People often ask me why I support Fianna Fáil, and want to know whether I would still support them if I wasn't born into the Party. The short answer is yes, but explaining it can often be difficult. Firstly, to me it makes eminent sense that people generally follow the politics of their parents. Most generations go through similar social and economic circumstances as their parents, albeit usually at a slightly wealthier level. It is normal, therefore, that your political outlook and opinions would not be too dissimilar to those of your parents. The reasons my parents trusted Fianna Fáil are more or less the same reasons that I do.

So why do I support them and not another political party? Well, as you can see, I don't have any time for political ideology; left or right is irrelevant when compared to the question of right or wrong. Let me put it another way altogether. Suppose you were a major corporate organisation and you had to appoint a new chief executive, what would you do? You would start by reviewing CVs, looking at the candidates' records, looking to see if they had a successful track record. Then you would interview them, chat to them, find out if they would fit in, decide if their personality would give your firm what it is looking for. You would never be concerned with whether they were left-wing or right-wing; the question would be, could they get the best results in the circumstances? I believe politics has a lot to do with personality and there is nothing wrong with that. People vote for the person and party they trust to do the job. There is no point having great policies but not having the ability to implement them.

I know everyone supports their own party for different reasons. I believe in Fianna Fáil because they have always most closely expressed my feelings on the majority of issues. I might not agree with every single policy, but that's what being in a party is about. I trust the personnel that have represented and continue to represent the Party, and I believe they are the most experienced and most capable. It's funny, but each party in Ireland seems to attract people of different personalities. Whether you trust these personalities or not is up to you.

Fianna Fáil is seen as larger than life, relatively exciting, nationalistic, schemers willing to do whatever it takes to get a job done, ready to deal with the devil himself, and at the same time proud and pragmatic. Fine Gael tends to be principled, educated and academic in approach, adhering strictly to the rules and unwilling to compromise on those for any reason, no matter how good; Fine Gaelers are also seen as reserved, bitter and realistic. Labour is ideological, willing to work on solutions, fond of debating issues even if it delays necessary action, slow to adapt but hard working. These are generalisations but they go a long way to describing the personality of our main parties. And, in terms of personality, you can see why one party would always find it difficult to support the other.

Growing up, I was always taught a number of things. Ireland was a country to be proud of and being Irish was something to hold dear. Rules should always be obeyed but can never be seen as the last word, because any rule will always have a loophole or problem. You must be willing to bend them if necessary for the common good, but not break them. Economic success is paramount to every individual and therefore you cannot take gambles on ideologies. Politics is a cruel game and if you aren't willing to play hard then you shouldn't be playing at all. Live in the real world and work to get results; make the best of whatever situation you find. Believe in yourself and be confident no matter what anyone else thinks. With those lessons embedded in my head, my natural home was always going to be Fianna Fáil.

In terms of policy, I would always favour the route of democratic and constitutional nationalism that Fianna Fáil expressed. Like the

Party, my views and reaction to events in the north have varied from outrage and anger on behalf of Catholics, to disinterest and even the odd nod of agreement with unionists. I always agreed with the idea of taking state privatisation on a case by case basis. I agreed with tax hikes and budget cuts when the country had no option but to enforce them, and I agreed with low tax and encouragement to enterprise once the economy recovered. I still favour taxes on individual items rather than blanket income taxes, let people call them 'stealth taxes' or otherwise. I believe the best way to help the poor is to encourage investment and provide work, rather than taxing the rich to a point where they leave, because then the poor are left even worse off. It's easy to say in an election that you hate the rich and they should be tackled, but the reality is if you try to destroy the rich they will survive and move elsewhere, and the ones who suffer will be the poor. Nonetheless it is the solemn duty of all those in power to look after workers and provide a voice and means for those who don't have them.

I am not going to patronise members of other parties by outlining why they support their parties, but if you ask them you will find that they do so for equally valid reasons. They just believe in a different approach, but most of all they simply trust different people to do the job.

There was no doubt that election fever was in the air in early 1997. Fianna Fáil was feeling confident. After some years of stumbling around post 1994, the Party had begun to find its feet. Bertie was making the Party his own and they had plenty to hit the government with, as oppositions often do. Biggest of these was the stalled Northern peace process. When Albert went, they all said it's bigger than any one man and that the process could survive his departure, but it bloody well couldn't. The IRA ceasefire collapsed and Reynold's guiding hand was desperately missed. But many people felt that if anyone could save it, it was going to be Bertie.

Best of all, though, was the fact that we were going to have a summer election, and you can't possibly imagine the smile that can bring to the face of a weary canvasser. No more freezing your hands on icy gates, getting soaked stumbling from door to door, and dropping cards as you fumble with them through gloves that do nothing to warm your fingers. Looking like a right pleb, hopping from foot to foot on the doorstep of an awkward customer, vainly trying to keep warm and dry but looking like you're a performing monkey. This time it could be mild weather and even some warm sunshine – campaigning in teeshirts, oh, what fun! Doing what any self-respecting single fella in politics does, I took two weeks holidays so as I could enjoy the election.

You might wonder why, after all the revelations about Haughey and the fact that there were several tribunals investigating planning matters, we could be so upbeat. It's hard to explain but that was the way it was. We saw the point that many commentators were missing. No one had any time for corruption, people want to see culprits dealt with. However, it is also true that good honest people should not be made to pay for the crimes of those who abused the system and in Fianna Fáil just as in Fine Gael and other parties, while there were some who milked the system, by and large they were made up of honest and hard-working individuals. The electorate was not interested in punishing politicians who had a good name and record just because someone else they knew didn't. The electorate was concerned with good government, and while they were outraged at some of the shenanigins that had gone on in the past they believed, as did all of us involved on the ground, that those days were thankfully gone and it was now a question of whether you believed the present day politicians were capable of doing a job for the country.

I went back up to Dundalk for a day, which was great, just getting to see all the old Fianna Fáilers up there. Then I was posted to the HQ media centre, doing media monitoring. Sounds exciting, doesn't it? Well, it's not the worst job, but not exactly riveting either, especially on a sunny afternoon. Effectively there was a myriad of radio and television sets, each one tuned to a different station. Every

news bulletin was recorded, so it was my job to jump up, press play and record, then replay it the tape and give a synopsis of the bulletin or programme and record the length of time we got. The idea was to ensure that we got as much airtime as everyone else. I fed my information back to a guy who compiled a similar report from other media, and it was all put on a central computer and was then fed to the PR gurus downstairs to deal with. At least it made for a trendy-sounding job, and, sure, wandering around Fianna Fáil's election HQ you'd never know who you might meet. Bertie himself popped up and had a chat with us one evening.

As it happened, I was down in Longford for Bertie's visit a matter of days later, and of course Bertie recognised me and said, 'Sure, this fella is workin' in headquarters.'

'I know,' Albert replied, 'sure, he does be everywhere.' I got a few jealous glances for that, this whippersnapper who everyone seemed to know – more importantly, everyone wanted to know what the bloody hell young Fallon was doing in HQ.

It was a different type of election in Longford, this time out. Albert was no longer in the ascendancy and it was strange not to be campaigning for a minister anymore. The opposition were going all out to try pull back his vote; there were even those in Fianna Fáil trying to pull at his vote, too. But Reynolds had a well-oiled machine and it had no bother dispersing the opposition, no matter where it came from. I got back into the normal election stuff like putting stickers on envelopes and folding letters, wonderful fun, I know, but someone has to be willing to do it. But it was a learning experience, too, sitting with people like Mickey Doherty and Noel Hanlon, running through the adverts and polls and whatever else came up. Tom Donlon the Comhairle Dáil Ceantar secretary, ran the show in those days, making sure everyone was where they should be when they should be, and keeping all the cumainn sweet, which is no small task.

Ógra Fianna Fáil was strong at the time too; people like Eileen McLoughlin, Marie Ward and Tony Flaherty had given it a very strong base. I usually avoided Ógra like the plague – every time I came into contact with it someone seemed to be having a row, but the Longford one seemed a well-run operation and Eileen cajoled me into signing up. Most of us Ógra members were used like para-troopers, dropped into an area that needed extra canvassers on any given day, so you could find yourself discussing the state of the roads up in the wilds of north Longford one day, and discussing the finer parts of national policy in the more refined south Longford the next.

We had a fair idea of how things stood nationally from Fianna Fáil's internal polls. Which is a system I'm going to break the secret code on and tell you all about.

As a pollster, you would get a call from HQ asking you to go to a hotel in, let's say, Cavan the following Saturday. Everyone would meet up and have a cup of tea, and then you would be assigned to a local driver and given a copy of the register of electors with a number of names ticked. The driver takes this list and transports you to the house, keeping his car out of sight. You have a sample ballot paper under your arm and you ask the person to fill it out confidentially, and then to answer some questions as to what the important issues of the day are. You don't tell them that you are from a political party, you just say it's a polling company (that's not really a lie), and most people couldn't be arsed about confidentiality anyway. They tell you who on the ballot paper should get the vote 'and that's that'. Very few care about whether people know the way they vote or not, but I bet they would care a little more if they had known who I was at the time.

But before you go off screaming blue murder about corruption or breach of trust, I always gave the person the ballot paper and an envelope, and told them to fill it confidentially and seal the envelope, but very few of them ever did. They would all proudly say, 'Oh, I don't care, it doesn't matter to me. I'll tell you now.'

The drivers, local men and women, could be shocked or pleas-antly surprised at times to discover what way a person was inclined to vote. But, to their eternal honour, I never had a driver ask to open a sealed envelope when we had one, and we never did open one either.

Often times, someone would be marked on the register and the driver would say, 'Ah, I know how they'll vote. Here, let's go to this fella instead.' But while there was no harm in that, there were those who tried so hard they did us no favours. 'Oh, Jaysus, don't go near him, he's a Blueshirt. I'll tell you, I know a good Fianna Fáil man; we'll go and ask him.' So much for a representative cross-section, and you would have to argue with the driver if you were to stick to the plan.

Meeting people during a campaign is a great experience. Sometimes it was too good. There was the lovely young lady in Cavan who answered the door in her dressing gown and invited me in, made me coffee, and had the most wonderful conversation with me. I can tell you, I didn't want to leave, but my driver's heating wasn't working so well and I felt bad leaving him in the car for as long as I did. And, of course, Mother Ireland and my duty to Fianna Fáil were calling.

People might not always have been so nice, but they were endlessly interesting. When I went to seek out one old man's views on the state of politics, he raised his walking stick to me and told me he was Fianna Fáil and didn't care 'whether it vexed or pleased you', and he had no time for media people like me with our polls. The list could go on endlessly. But, on a serious note, one thing did disturb me: there was a huge amount of elderly people who, when I called to their door, never asked why I had no car, never asked for ID, but just welcomed me into their homes to answer the questions. It was lovely that they did it and made me feel very welcome, but I could have been anyone, and with so many of them willing to be so friendly I eventually stopped taking their hospitality and would tell them not to be so trusting. It still breaks my heart to hear of intruders breaking into elderly people's homes, when I think of how open and honest those people are, and then one day to have that trust violated.

Off the streets and into the studio for the mandatory appearances on *Questions and Answers*. Now that is a great programme for the activists. Political parties are always asking people to take up the audience tickets; in fact 99 per cent of the audience are political plants of one sort or another. You simply got a call to go out to RTÉ, and off you would go. The great thing about attending anything out in Montrose is the fact that they supply the audience with free wine beforehand; that's why you see so many glassy eyes and happy smiling faces in the audiences. (The drink they give to the crowd who attend *Winning Streak* must be a lot stronger; I reckon they must feed them poitín all day to get them to carry out those antics in front of the nation.) Anyway, for *Questions and Answers*, you all sit in a room writing down possible questions and you chat to whoever is close to you, maybe even share a pen. Only a complete novice would ask someone else who they were there to represent; there is no point ruining the conversation by discovering that you are political enemies and about to enter the arena of death that is the *Questions and Answers* studio. Eventually RTÉ selects and rephrases the question and whoever was closest to it gets to ask it. Scientific stuff.

When the discussion gets underway, it's your job to ensure that you get your hand up and make a salient point, while trying to hide the fact that you represent anybody. If you are not careful, presenter John Bowman will 'out' you and tell everyone who you are! More importantly, it's your job to support your politician by clapping everything he or she says. You must out-clap the supporters of other parties in the audience. Good job you have plenty of wine inside you. What comes across to viewers as people endorsing a point well made is actually a load of political activists vying to outdo one another.

Meanwhile, back on the ranch, the election was moving at a ferocious pace. It was also fun, because confidence in the Party was high. As the campaign progressed, it became evident that neither side was going to win out, but we were safe in the knowledge that if we didn't make it with the PDs we could get a few independents, and no better man than Bertie to negotiate a deal.

In Longford, the count itself was an unusual experience. There was something surreal about the fact that Albert was not going to be in cabinet when it was over, even though the situation looked good for the Party. Unfortunately, it wasn't going well for the PDs – there was even a rumour that Mary Harney had lost her seat, which turned out to be untrue, of course, but she had not polled as well as one might expect. Once the tallies were in and I had played my part in the number crunching, I headed home to catch a better picture of what was happening nationally, stopping only at the door to smile and nod at dejected Tom Fox supporters as they saw their seat slip away. Hey, don't blame me, they started it; I just like to finish things.

That night, as the television droned out result after result, I had a strange feeling sitting there at home with the folks. It was almost like the changing of the guard – for the first time it seemed like it was me who was responsible for jotting down numbers, and like it was me who was the important figure now. Mam and Dad were no less interested, but undoubtedly they took a back seat and expected that I could do the running now. You spend your early life wishing you could be just like your folks and then suddenly one day you are, and it's nothing like what you imagined.

In our house we always enjoyed predicting seats and working out numbers based on the tally figures. It was the only time I took an interest in anything remotely mathematical. Mind you, it's not easy – you have to know what you're doing. Geography and local knowledge are the key but it also requires a firm understanding of proportional representation (PR). We viewed Ireland's voting system with a certain amount of distrust.

It is generally considered fair, and it allows for all viewpoints to be represented in some way. It means that even though you may not get a huge vote or be the most popular candidate, you can still take a seat based on the support you do have. It ensures that politics remains competitive and that politicians must look after their constituents. It allows a broad spectrum of views, reflecting society at large, to be expressed in the Dáil. However, the system also brings problems.

In a presidential election it is a disaster, as there is no multi-seat business, so the most popular candidate, the person who is the majority's first choice, may not always be elected. In a general election, small parties have a distinct advantage in picking up seats in large, five-seat constituencies. By favouring small parties like this, PR helps them hold the balance of power, and you are left with a situation where the representatives of a small minority of the people are dictating to the majority. Proportional representation does not make for stable government as there is such a broad range of parties that no one party can hold control; as a result there is an over-reliance on deals and pacts which can too often falter. And the impact of multi-seat constituencies is often to make politicians more concerned with their constituency business than looking after the interests of the country.

So, while our household respected the system, we disliked it, because it continually conspired to work against the larger parties in the Dáil, and seemed hell-bent on destroying Fianna Fáil's hopes of the overall majority. The larger a party gets, the more difficult it is to win extra seats under PR.

The great thing about it, though, is that if you do manage to understand our system and the use of the single transferable vote (STV), then you can go anywhere in the world and their electoral system will seem like child's play. We undoubtedly operate one of the most complex voting mechanisms possible, and in truth we are forced to admit that many of our own voters don't even know how it works. For those of you who are not electoral nerds like myself, a brief outline is probably appropriate, if for no other reason than that we should understand when we go to vote.

A constituency has a number of seats, let's say four. The total number of votes cast is counted and divided by the number of seats, and this figure plus 1 equals the quota – the number you need to reach to be elected.

The voter marks his candidates 1, 2, 3, 4 on the ballot in order of preference, and all the No. 1 votes are counted first. Let's imagine that one candidate polls well over the quota; now there is a surplus which must be distributed. Our hypothetical candidate is 2,000 votes over the quota, so his No. 2 votes are looked at and counted, and if another candidate gets, lets say 50 per cent of the total No. 2 votes, then 1,000 votes are added to his first preferences. In reality, not every vote can be counted a second time, so this figure is arrived at by checking random batches and counting the No. 2 votes in these batches. The votes gained in this manner may or may not be sufficient to elect a second candidate; either way, the next step will be the elimination of the candidate with the lowest votes. This elimination must provide enough votes to get someone else over the quota. In other words, if the quota was 8,000 and the nearest candidate had 7,000 votes already, but the lowest candidate in the field only has 500 votes, then he or she must be eliminated and so must the next lowest candidate. Their votes are then distributed according to preference.

This process continues until all the seats are filled. In practice, it often gets a lot more complex. For instance, if a candidate is eliminated, but the No. 2 vote is for someone who is already elected or has been eliminated previously, then, rather than waste the voter's selection, the candidate's No. 3 vote is counted. And if after several rounds of this a candidate is eliminated, then the votes which were given to him from other candidates in earlier rounds must be counted and transferred to whoever was next on the list of preferences on that vote, so the counting moves on down through the choices the voter made on the ballot paper. If it sounds complex, that's because it is. And then there are the recounts, when everything has to be checked all over again.

You might think that you would need to be a computer to figure all that out and avoid errors – that's what the rest of the world usually thinks too – but in Ireland we couldn't be trusting computers, sure we'll work it all out near enough to right in our heads. The old attachment to mental arithmetic still holds strong.

Anyway, a short couple of weeks after the 1997 election the deal was done. Fianna Fáil, the PDs and a few independents. Back in business; back where we belonged. I took another day off work to see the new government take over. What joy, standing on the Dáil plinth again with Mickey Doherty, everybody who passed knew him. He had a long chat with Jackie Healy Rae, who was being cheered on by hordes of schoolchildren brought up especially for the day. Healy Rae was one of the independents that the new government was relying on for support. He was a former Fianna Fáil man who had left the Party because he was not selected as a candidate and then ran successfully as an independent. Jackie is one of the great characters of Irish politics and has a lot more political acumen than he is often given credit for. Needless to say though, I still couldn't condone his leaving the Party. If it's what you believe then you support it whether you are the person the Party chooses or not.

Leinster House was crammed once more; the good times could flow. Donie Cassidy was grinning like a cheshire cat and telling me how this could be the best government ever. I went up to Albert's office with Mickey Doherty and Bennie Reid, though the great man himself wasn't there, just us three and his secretary. It was a small office and I couldn't help but think of how the days of grandeur had passed. We watched the events on a screen in the office, saw Jackie Healy Rae make his maiden speech, and at some stage Mickey dozed off, having seen it all so many times before.

I decided to take a wander and see what was happening else-where. Discussions were taking place all along the corridors as people tried to guess the make-up of the cabinet. In the end I gra-vitated toward my second home, the Dundalk crowd, who were in buoyant mood – after a strong performance as Party whip, Dermot Ahern was virtually guaranteed a seat at cabinet. In the end, he got Social, Community and Family affairs, and though we had all hoped for foreign affairs, nonetheless he was a minister and that's all that mattered. Up in the whip's office the joy was overwhelming – Dermot's lovely wife, Maeve, and their children were ecstatic, and already Pearse O'Hanrahan was on the phone, arranging the homecoming celebration.

After a few drinks and a hell of a good time, I left Leinster House late that night, myself and Dermot's secretary, Christine Maguire, humming 'Time to Say Goodbye' as we walked after a tired and dejected-looking Dick Spring. Like many others, he had stuck the knife into Fianna Fáil, only for it to come back and haunt him. As he got into his car, I waved him goodbye, and he waved back, I thought, 'What a shame. I used to think he was OK once.'

Back at work, things were very sweet – nothing like having the blood of victory dripping from your lips when you are facing a few famished Blueshirts. I immediately went into overdrive for my old pet project, the new building at St Mel's in Longford. It had been shoved right down the list by the rainbow coalition, but now its time had come. With the help of Christy Mannion, who was appointed as an adviser to education minister Mícheál Martin, we were going to get it done. We did, too, and the day of the grand opening, when Fr Garvey in his speech thanked me for all my help, was one of the proudest moments in my life. I never pass that fabulous new building but I thank God for having been in a position to help it along. These are the real benefits, the reason why everyone should be involved in politics.

In the meantime, I got a phone call from Christine inviting me to go to Dundalk for Dermot's homecoming, and I was only too happy to say yes. I agreed I'd meet the cavalcade at Drogheda train station and travel in one of the cars from there. What a thrill it was being in that convoy as we rolled into Dundalk, stopping in Blackrock where the public were out in force. We went to the hotel and had one of the best nights I can remember, especially after meeting up with a few others from the old college cumann.

The tribunals continued right throughout the period, and there was no doubt that some of their revelations were shocking. None more so than the questions being asked of Ray Burke. Bertie Ahern had appointed him to cabinet on returning to government, which had surprised some people. Certainly it was not something that sat easy with those of us from Longford. Albert Reynolds had sacked him, and he had been a thorn in the side throughout Albert's tenure. We knew he didn't like our side of the Party and he had been only too willing to stick the boot in when things were crumbling in 1994. While we felt some sympathy for him due to the fact that he was under sustained attack during a family bereavement, I would be lying if I said that I, or many of those I knew, shed too many tears when he resigned. However, we certainly never suspected that he was receiving large sums of money as donations or otherwise, and the revelation did shock us to the core. Fianna Fáil party members felt more betrayed than anyone by the actions of some politicians, but our belief that the Party itself was still good and was still the main vehicle for change and advancement in the country and the economy held firm. Just because some people let you down, that's no excuse for abandoning the cause of what you believe. It's still worth fighting for.

Albert Reynolds was still the TD for Longford, but he had his eyes on another prize. The presidency. There had to be an election as Mary Robinson's second term was coming to a close. However, yet again she managed to hurt us. Having fought tooth and nail for the job in 1990 and considering all Brian Lenihan had to go through, it really galled us that Robinson decided to pack in the job of president some months before her term was up. She got a better offer from the UN and, as far as we could see, it felt like she was saying that being president was no big deal, the UN was more important and if that meant you had to leave the job a bit early then so be it, who cares about being first citizen anyway?

Reynolds was well placed for the Fianna Fáil nomination. We obviously supported him, we knew it would cause a by-election if he was successful, but in Longford we also had no fear but that we would win a by-election. As time went on however the picture of other candidates became clearer, former Eurovision winner, Dana, wanted to run, Mary Banotti the Fine Gael MEP was running, and then Labour brought in Adi Roche the campaigner on aid for Chernobyl victims. Things began to change. Outside of Longford Party people started to get afraid. If Reynolds ran it was going to bring up all the controversy about Beef tribunals, the collapse of the government in 1994 and all that stuff. Now while Albert did not have any case to answer on these fronts, we knew from the experience with Lenihan that certain people in politics and the media would try to twist it to say that he had. Mary McAleese entered the frame for the nomination. She was from the north, and was a confident communicator and a cool customer under pressure. She was female and had no baggage.

Bertie Ahern said that he supported Albert but it was up to the parliamentary party to vote on their selection. In the end Albert lost. Everyone felt he had been shafted. While the Party publicly said it wanted him, privately it was decided that McAleese would make for an easier campaign. The day of the nomination vote I was working in the bank in College Green. I heard the news and just decided to walk up to Leinster House, as it happened I arrived as Albert and some other ministers and TDs who supported him were coming out of the gates on Kildare street. I was first over to shake the hand of a visibly shocked Albert as the group walked over to Buswells Hotel for a press conference. I didn't go in, it felt too bad to be honest. I stood outside on the steps and chatted with MEP Brian Crowley, who was annoyed and disappointed. We bemoaned what was becoming of candidate selection and the fact that Albert lost on the basis of what might be said or accusations that might be laid against him rather than being judged on his ability for the job.

The ensuing 1997 presidential election wasn't the most exciting. Adi Roche collapsed at the polls in part because Labour did not have enough organisation and could not get enough people out on the ground to promote her. Further evidence that what happened in 1990 was more down to Lenihan's problems with the media than any rush of votes to the Labour candidate. Mary McAleese was a brilliant candidate and dealt with everything that was thrown at her. She did prove to be a great choice. Fianna Fáil regained the presidency with considerable ease and she went on to become probably our most successful and popular president ever.

I loved being part of the whole political game, but in truth my own career in politics wasn't going anywhere fast and I was beginning to wonder if I even wanted one. Longford Fianna Fáil was having a bit of a downer, too. Tom Donlon told me we needed something, even something small to lift everyone again, to get them looking forward.

At the Árd Fheis that year I began to have an idea. The Árd Fheis elects fifteen people to the árd comhairle, the Party's national executive – in the best and most imaginative of Fianna Fáil traditions, called the Committee of Fifteen. I decided I should be on it. I was in no doubt that getting elected wasn't easy, but I had all the confidence of youth and figured I could handle it. I was well settled in at the bank now, and had my own car, a big white 1991 Nissan Sunny. The girls in the bank baptised the car 'Johnny's babemobile', and how I wished it were true, but I didn't pull any more women with it than I used to do before. Running for election wasn't going to help me on that score either.

8

BORN TO RUN

The time had come to stick my neck out. The Árd Comhairle election was a challenge I felt I needed, and one that might give people in Longford Fianna Fáil a boost – after all, it is meant to be an opportunity for the local cumainn to elect representatives directly to this august body. Cumainn had a free choice as to who they voted for. Someone from Cork or Mayo could vote for you just the same as someone from Longford or Westmeath. This made the task difficult, because while some counties could have three or four hundred cumainn, Longford had only thirty-three. This gives you some idea of the uphill battle I faced coming from a county with such a small base. It meant I was going to have to spend a lot of time on the road trying to get votes in other counties before voting took place at the next Árd Fheis.

I started campaigning pretty much as soon as the 1997 Árd Fheis was over. The support from the Longford machine was spectacular, especially from stalwarts like Tom Donlon, Bennie Reid and Mickey Doherty. Campaigning was going to take a long time and a lot of effort. I needed organisation, I needed to get my name out there and let people know that this was my patch, and I had to convince people that I was the right man for the job.

Other than that my life revolved mainly around work, drink and trying to find love. I kept looking in all the likely locations: O'Neill's straight after work, Quinn's in Drumcondra, Hedigan's in Glasnevin, and the mother of them all, McGowan's of Phibsboro. If you haven't discovered it yet, then my advice is don't. It's Dublin's answer to the 'House of the Rising Sun'. Once you get in the habit of going in there, then you will end up there seven nights a week. There's a DJ who plays slow sets, just the way you remember it. There are nurses, teachers, gardaí and lonely country girls, with the odd Dub mixed in to make it more exotic. Myself and my fellow lodger, James O'Dea from Loughrea, spent many a wasted night in there. It's all very well sitting down in front of the television to watch *Fair City*, with your foot twitching as you clasp that cup of tea. Yes, it's all very well indeed, until someone mentions going to McGowan's. Now you think of having a pint instead of the tea, you think of all the craic that's probably happening down there right now. It eats at you all the way through *Fair City*. You think of the last time, the short skirts, the knee high boots and eventually, labouring under some vain illusion that it's fate telling you tonight is your night, you jump up grab your jacket and say 'All right, come on to fuck the acting is shite in this anyway.' Rarely do you think of the walk home in the rain, the dry bacon-and-egg sandwich from the Shell station at three in the morning – for some reason you never even think of the next morning, not when you're going to McGowan's.

In general, there were plenty of parties. My old friend Ciarán McGuinness was doing nursing over in Beaumont Hospital. A greater love hath no man than to become a nurse for his friends. Being a male nurse is a very tough job, but being a male nurse's friend is bloody great. Nurses parties were held regularly in Break for the Border, and there was any number of house parties. In a class of nurses, you could have seventy females to five fellas. Talk about striking it lucky! There was always some you were either interested in, or they were interested in you, or there was at least some form of scandal at any rate. One thing for sure, life was never boring.

Months just seemed to whizz by, and why not: I was having a ball. Women, money in my pocket, pubs to visit – and running an election campaign in my spare time. So, you're thinking, I must have been having the time of my life? Well, in one sense I was; in another, far from it. It was also one of the loneliest periods I have experienced. Yes, there were plenty of girls to keep me amused, but nothing that lasted longer than a couple of weeks at best. I was finding the city a particularly alien animal and, to be honest, could have done with a girlfriend or someone just to share time with. Dubs will probably find this difficult to understand, but it's a story that's all too familiar to many culchies. You're living away from home, but not abroad, so no one is really interested in how you are 'adjusting'. You don't get the comfort of people understanding that you are in what is, in fact, a foreign city. It's no great shock to say that Dublin is more akin to London than it ever will be to Longford, or any other county in the Republic for that matter. Dublin is London without the style, but it's still Ireland so people aren't interested in hearing you moan. After all, you get home most weekends, don't you?

Yes, but in many ways that makes it worse. I loved getting home, despite being stuck in tailbacks for hours as I drove out of the city. I needed to get home, but the problem was that Sunday came around far too quickly. I worried that my abiding memory of my parents would be the image of them in my rear-view mirror, as they stood on that little country road waving me off. Knowing in my heart and soul that I didn't want to be going and they didn't want me to go either. However, spending a weekend in Dublin on your own is even worse. Sure, Friday night is great. Saturday isn't usually as good but you sleep off the hangover and then try to round up anyone at all to go on the razz that night. Sunday morning you wake up like you have gone twelve rounds with Tyson, and that's when reality hits you. Kris Kristofferson's 'Sunday Morning Coming Down' pretty much sums up being on your own in a city on a Sunday; 'and there's nothing short of dying, half as lonesome as the sound, of the sleeping city sidewalks, with Sunday morning coming down'.

The bank wasn't the worst paymaster in the world, but in the new Celtic Tiger that was just beginning to bare its teeth, they were falling behind fast. I wasn't destitute, I did have a bit of cash to spend, but there was never a shortage of ways to spend it. The election was also set to cost me a bomb. Between petrol, travel, flyers, stickers, it was going to be a tall order.

Summer is usually the time to lighten your mood and no better way to kick it off than the World Cup, France 1998. Ireland didn't qualify, but for the true football fan that was not a problem, especially for league of Ireland fans anyway – the players we supported week in week out never even got a look-in Ireland's friendlies, never mind competitive matches. When Ireland aren't in the world cup, you can sit back and enjoy the cream of the football action. We were generally finished work in time to pop into O'Neill's for the second half of the second match of the day. After that we might hang on and watch the next game, and then we would need to analyse the match and talk. Drink, drink and more drink. Ulster Bank, College Green, was filled with sore heads for the entire month of the world cup. I knew it was time to start copping on when my housemate, O'Dea, who was a much harder drinker than I ever was, said to me, 'Jaysus, I was fierce worried about you during the World Cup, you were on the lash every fuckin' night, fallin' home in some state.' For him to have noticed, I must have been bad. And I was. One night I made it home but couldn't face the stairs, and fell asleep right there on the steps.

But I was doing one thing right, and that was organising my campaign. I was helping Kevin McGuinness in his campaign to be elected to the executive through Ógra, which helped me garner at least some of the Ógra votes, which I would not usually get due to my rather old-fashioned view of the Party. We combined going to watch Longford play Wexford in the football championship with a quick chat with Lisa McDonald on the possibility of mentioning our names down around that part of the country. Lisa was running for the Committee of Fifteen herself and was a former chair of the Kevin Barry cumann in UCD, she would go on to be a FF candidate in the future. I visited Laois twice and was overwhelmed by the reception I got; I made many friends there and I'll never forget them.

On the second occasion, we arrived to a meeting of their comhairle Dáil, where the first thing up for discussion was the fact that a cancer unit had been located in Tullamore rather than Portlaoise hospital. It was a heated debate, and I remember Gerry McEvoy who travelled with me from Longford Ógra, leaning over to me and saying, 'Jaysus, we would be delighted if we had any kind of hospital in Longford.' It was true, of course, Longford was the only county in the Midland Health Board area with no specific hospital; instead we shared Mullingar with Westmeath.

Brian Cowen, Minister for Health at the time, arrived halfway through the meeting. Boy, did skin and hair fly then – you don't want to criticise Brian Cowen, I can tell you. He laid out the reasons the decision was made, dared anyone to suggest it was a personal decision, and pretty much ended the argument there and then. A cancer unit had to be accessible to everyone, he said, and the health board decided on Tullamore because Portlaoise was too far from the other end of the region. He looked over at us and said, 'I can't help it, but people above in Longford die from cancer, too. What would you like me to tell these lads from Longford – to go home tonight and tell everyone that they will have to travel to the other end of the region for care?'

Jaysus, Brian, I thought, that's all I fuckin' need. I came here to get votes and at this rate you'll get me bloody lynched. Thankfully it didn't turn out that way; the issue was debated but, once the case was laid out, those present had enough political savvy to understand its merits. The Party people in Laois are among the most able and friendliest I have met anywhere across the country. I knew, as all true Fianna Fáilers know, that Laois-Offaly wouldn't let me down.

The travelling wasn't easy, and getting time off work was next to impossible. Down and back in one night, it wasn't so bad when one of the lads agreed to come with me, but the nights on my own it was difficult to keep the eyes open at 3.30 a.m. heading back for Dublin, and there were more than a few scrapes. I was well on the way, though, and then I was blindsided by an unexpected problem.

Someone in the upper echelons of Ulster Bank went to my manager, Finbar Daly, and suggested that my running in this campaign was in contravention of head office instructions, a collection of rules by which bank employees are supposed to live their lives. Finbar called me in and explained the situation to me. He was a really good sort and a great guy to work for, and I knew it was the last thing he wanted to be talking to me about. He was actually interested in my campaign, in fact, but as a bank manager he had to apply the rules. He suggested I meet with a head guy down in George's Quay, and in the meantime he would explain that, in his opinion, there was no issue as regards my day-to-day work. But he looked again at the sentence which forbade an employee running for public or political office, and said, 'It does seem to block you, Johnny.' I admitted it didn't look good.

'What then for you?' Finbar asked. 'Presumably, if they say no, what will you have to do to get out of the campaign? I mean, will it cost you money now?'

I laughed. 'There is no question as to whether I'm running or not. The only question is whether I'm still a bank employee or not when the election comes round'.

I think he was shocked, but I was never in any doubt on the matter. Any organisation, no matter how moral or practical their reasons, that actively discourages employees from doing their civic duty – to be political and be involved in serving their state, in whatever capacity – was not worthy of my time. Any such organisation would get a rather rude piece of my mind for imposing such a rule, and they would have been foolish to think that I would let things lie at that.

I was given an appointment to meet this guy in George's Quay. He was a big name in the bank, but the fact that I can't even remember his name shows the frame of mind I was in going to the meeting. Respect for the bank or its rules was not high on my agenda. We went into a room and I explained what the position was: that I was running for office in the Fianna Fáil party and I felt it important to do so. To be fair to the man, he looked bemused by the whole situation. I don't think that deep down he believed this was even an issue. I knew I was on a winner when he told me his father had been a cumann chairman out in Sandyford – at least I think it was Sandyford but it could have been Stillorgan, either way it amounts to the same thing. He told me that he wished me luck and thanked me for meeting with him, and that he hoped it hadn't coloured my opinion of the bank, but that these were just procedures that had to be followed. There was no problem with me being a candidate, he said. I was delighted. To be honest, I did not fancy giving up my job, even though that's what I would have done.

There was to be more shock news on the job front a little later, though. Everyone in the trust company was called to a meeting, where we were told that the bank was reassessing its business and, while all our jobs were safe, our work would be reorganised. The income tax section was to go. Finbar would take early retirement and would deal with all the existing clients from home. The payroll section was to be disbanded and clients would be advised to find new operators. Instead, the bank would expand the core business of wills and trusts and we would all be gainfully employed there. One person would be transferred out of the section, probably to branch banking.

The news came as such a shock that I sat down with Finbar, who opened an old bottle of whiskey and gave me a shot of it. OK, my job was safe, but all I knew was the payroll and tax sections. I didn't want to work on wills and trusts. I gave it a lot of thought over the coming days and decided I'd volunteer to be posted to another branch. What had I to lose? I hated Dublin. I had seen branch banking and I didn't mind it at all; I liked dealing with customers. I went in next day to Margaret O'Shea, who was taking over as manager, and asked if I could be the one transferred. She said that they would be very sorry to lose me, but if that was what I wanted, then it would be easier on everyone. Great! I was already becoming a little bit excited about the prospect of being sent to a new town, meeting new people, and even having a new chance of hoovering up another pocket of votes in advance of the election to the Committee of Fifteen.

Then Margaret called me in and said that she had put my proposal to her superior, but he had said no, because I was more experienced (even though I knew nothing of the work they were about to assign to me). It would be last in, first out; in other words, Stephen Galbraith would be the one to go. I felt so sorry for Stephen. He didn't want to move. He was a Dub and so was his girlfriend, and the thought of being moved to the lottery of branch banking didn't appeal to him. To be fair, he was moved to the bank's southern regional office and then onto a Dublin branch, and as far as I am aware the move never did him any harm; in fact, he made it work out well. But it was a bizarre decision. They could have appeased everyone by moving me. But I was stuck in Dublin, fed up with work, and thoroughly pissed off.

Now, as the only person who dealt with payroll, I was overseeing the transfer of our clients to other payroll companies and accountants. In other words, I was on the phone chatting to several potential employers a day. I mean, that's the equivalent of letting a priest into the Playboy mansion. It doesn't matter how happy I might have been (and that wasn't very happy), there were sure to be offers that could turn my head. I mentioned this to Margaret, who laughed and asked why would I want to move. Considering I was on £13,000 a year, I thought the question was a bit foolish. I said that if I got an offer of £20,000 I'd have to go. 'I don't think there's any fear of that,' she told me.

As the days went on, I began negotiating with clients. Liam Ryan of Ryan Glennon and Company rang me up on one of those days and asked me to drop out to them for a chat if I was interested in moving jobs. To be perfectly honest, I was talking to KPMG, Cara, Quantum and other bigger names, so I wasn't overly enthusiastic. I had never heard of Ryan Glennon at the time and figured they wouldn't be able to match some of the offers I had received already. When the day came to drop out to them after work I really didn't want to go. It was a damp evening, I was tired and fed up and just wanted to go home rather than head out to the depths of the southside – Ranelagh, an area that I was completely unfamiliar with. A girl who worked with me, Sinead, persuaded me. 'Look, Johnny, what have you got to lose? It's one bloody evening and no big deal if they're not what you want, but you might as well go and see.' I decided I'd better do it, and in the end I was glad I did. They made a better offer than anyone else, an offer that meant a £5,000 increase in salary. I liked them, their approach, their professionalism, the people I met, and above all the lack of red tape and strict procedures that I found so stifling in the bank. One week later, I handed in my notice to Margaret. She looked surprised.

'Don't tell me you got offered £20k?' she said.

'No,' I said, 'but near enough.'

She shook her head. 'I must be missing something in these pay-roll jobs; there seems to be great opportunities in them.'

In the end, it showed how life can turn and change so quickly. If the bank had let me transfer, I would probably still be there today. As Jarvis Cocker sang, 'Life could have been very different, but then something changed.'

I had reason to celebrate, and when my old friend Mick Lennon rang me to say he had an invitation to go to France to play at a commemoration of the 1798 rebellion, I jumped at the chance. His girlfriend Lorraine came with us too. We headed for Saint Nabord, where we were put up by a local family who were more than kind to us. We met a load of councillors from Mayo there too (handy for the old Committee of Fifteen votes) and made some good contacts with the Irish Embassy in Paris.

The French were mad for Irish music. They didn't seem to understand our need for sleep, though. We were asked to play in a makeshift pub set up in their community centre, and this went on until three in the morning. They weren't great at keeping the rhythm of the music, but in fairness to them they were all drunk, even the Mayor up and dancing around along with the entire population of this little town. They fed us a steady stream of canned Guinness and seemed to want us to live up to the stereotypical Irish billing. We didn't let them down. We drank until we couldn't see straight and played until our fingers blistered and bled.

We were exhausted, but when the cream of the local French female talent asked us to go with them to the disco, we thought it would have been ungentlemanly to refuse. Caught up in the moment, we had a ball, and I met a lovely French girl who I knew I shouldn't encourage, but what the hell, I dived straight in and made the most of the opportunity. Ah, fuck it. I'm a man. That's what we do.

The following morning our hosts were knocking on the door at 7 a.m. to get us up for a tour of the area. We marched zombie like onto a bus. Mick and Lorraine promptly fell asleep and snored right through the tour guide's commentary. Trying to be polite, I forced myself to stay awake, and in fairness we were treated like lords and given the finest of meals and drink that they had to offer. When the bus arrived back we soon discovered that we were due to play music again, so I went off to source some plasters for my blisters, and when I came back found that the local youth had gathered around us again. My new girlfriend was there and ran over to me as soon as she saw me. I was rather embarrassed when she started to kiss me passionately in front of the lady from the embassy and a local priest.

The French were great, though. We got the impression that they looked on Parisians the same way as we look on the Dubs, so I suppose we connected as culchies. The night before we left, we went to a house where two girls who were mad into Mick lived with their mother. We sang for hours, everything from 'The Green Fields of France' to 'Frere Jacque'. It was also time for me to say goodbye to my girl. She gave me a present and everything, promised to write every week, and wanted to come to Ireland in the Summer. I knew it would all be different when I went home.

Johnny was on the high road again. It gave me a lift to have changed jobs in the run-up to the election, and now I began to cover a huge amount of the country, sometimes only meeting one or two people and sometimes a hundred, but I didn't care so long as people mentioned my name. The flyers were printed, the people in Longford were on the phones ringing contacts everywhere, Albert sent a letter of support. By the final week I was utterly shattered. It is only by taking part in a campaign like this that you really understand just how many people in Ireland are involved in politics, and how big the Fianna Fáil party is. The differences in opinion, background, social status, religious belief, geography can only be appreciated at this level, and you realise that all these diverse people are unified by one thing: Fianna Fáil. That the Party still manages to do this is bloody amazing.

To make matters worse for me, though, I developed the mother of all toothaches in the last fortnight before the Árd Fheis. I did everything to numb the pain and keep smiling, I was living on Lemsip and Solpadeine, dissolving the two together and knocking them back like lemonade at times. I didn't have time to go to the dentist but one night the pain got so bad I went to A&E in the Mater. It was a nightmare. Junkies, drunks, and the odd sick person all jammed in, fighting, shouting, and sleeping. I waited five hours to be seen and in the end the doctor said, 'Oh, it's dental, and I don't think we can do anything for the pain. Here are two paracetamol, and try to get some rest.' I mentally pictured shoving the paracetamol up his arse and sealing it with a kick, but to be fair it wasn't his area and it was my own fault for not getting to a dentist. So I went home and loaded up on Solpadeine again and took the paracetamol for good measure. My mother also sent me up some kind of stuff you rub on the tooth. I wasn't too sure what it was but I used that as well anyway.

At the end of the campaign I travelled to Navan. Meath is another county I love, and the Fianna Fáil organisation there is second to none. I made friends for life among them and they supported me wholeheartedly at the Árd Fheis. Johnny Brady, TD, introduced those of us who were Committee of Fifteen candidates to the meeting, and when he got to me he said, 'And there's Johnny Fallon. Now, whoever said that Fianna Fáil can't attract the young?' The crowd broke into applause and I knew that comment alone would keep me in their minds – it was the best drug I had yet been given for that bloody toothache. Exhausted, I travelled home to Longford that night. When I got in the door in the early hours I crumbled into an armchair by the fire. Mam and Dad fussed about me and for once I was glad of it. I felt I was now at the end of a very tough road but I had doubts in my mind even so. The pain in my jaw was dampening my confidence and I told my parents I was worried, considering that I needed at least 1,000 votes even to be in with a shout, and Longford could only deliver 66 votes on its own. At times like that it's always good to be among your own.

The big day finally arrived. I hadn't managed to get a dentist appointment, so I stocked up on painkillers and headed to the Árd Fheis. The buzz was amazing. We canvassed all through the opening on the Friday night and had a great team out early on Saturday morning. Retiring Councillor Paddy Farrell and his son Gerry came up to help out and they put their heart and soul into it; everyone from cumainn right across Longford lent a hand. They were all delighted to be back in a campaign, and they wanted to flex their muscles and see if their ability was all down to Albert or if they could actually get an unknown through a tough election.

Donie Cassidy was there doling out my flyers and drumming up votes at every opportunity. Mícheál Martin's adviser, Christy Mannion, another Ballymahon man, was wearing the sticker and keeping me in the mind of Cork voters. Agreements with fellow candidates Dara Calleary and John Watson were working well. Councillor Barney Steele and his wife Rita worked so hard I was actually worried for their own health! Mary Hanafin came up to me and said, 'Paddy Farrell has warned me not to let you down! But, come here, where did you get this team of people? That's some show you're putting on here today.' I had a brilliant team, and not least my parents. Standing and watching my father and mother canvass for me was an experience I could never forget. There was my father, meeting a former busman from his days in Dublin, and pulling in another pocket of votes. My aunt was mother superior in a convent in Ratoath, and another nun, Sr Mary Clement, ensured all her Fianna Fáil contacts from Wexford knew about me. As one of them said when they met me, 'The nuns told me to make sure I voted for you, and if you have the church behind you, you will be all right.' I was counting on their prayers too!

The help and support I received overawed me. Eileen McLoughlin, herself a former member of the executive, was keeping me posted and ensuring everyone had flyers and stickers and that everything was organised from my own point of view as well as the team. She never let me forget to eat, and got me to calm down during the day. Her confidence was infectious. Councillor Peter Kelly and Tony Flaherty kept sending in voters with my name in their minds, and Councillor Fintan Flood never ceased to amaze me by the sheer number of people he knew throughout the organisation. There were too many people for me to be able to mention them all, but the Longford organisation proved its worth and showed just how good they really were.

I shook hands with every voter who went into the stalls. Every so often, I met a group from Louth, Meath, Laois, Offaly, places where I knew I had good support, and it lifted the spirits and gave me energy. And then, when the voting was over, it felt weird. This thing had taken up a year of my life and now it was gone. In the meantime, relationships had suffered, I was no nearer than ever to finding a soul mate; in fact, I barely had the energy to try anymore. Was it going to be worth it?

As the votes were counted, little nuggets of information and whispers kept coming to the waiting candidates. Word spread quickly that Johnny Fallon was polling well. Galway had won the All-Ireland that year, and Deputy Seán Power, no stranger to sporting bets, came up to me and said, 'September was the month for Ja Fallon, and it looks like November will be for Johnny Fallon'. By the time the warm-up had started for the Taoiseach's address, Mary Hanafin, Beverly Cooper Flynn, Terry Leyden and a host of others were already congratulating me, saying it was a great performance, even though no official result had been announced.

I wouldn't let myself believe the result until I saw it in black and white. When I did I made my way down to my parents, who were sitting two rows from the front of the stage. I didn't want to obstruct people's view so I just leaned in to my father and said, '1,362 topped the poll in Leinster'. He nearly cried, and my own heart was ready to burst. My mother didn't know whether to stand up or sit down and was in a tizzy because she wanted to hug me. Suddenly everyone around began to tug at me and ask if I had made it, and when I told them I had they shook my hand and hugged me. I can't remember who was speaking on the podium at the time but they must have thought it odd that suddenly this little section of the crowd was breaking into hugs and handshakes.

I waited at the back of the hall to shake hands with delegates as they left. I wanted to thank them all. I was mobbed by a group of women from Tallaght who where thrilled that I was elected and were all over me. It was a feeling I will never forget to the day I die, and one that everyone should experience at least once in a lifetime.

I managed the following week to get to the dental hospital. The euphoria of being elected had almost killed the pain in the meantime. But when the dentist looked at the tooth and started talking about how difficult it would be to save it, the chances of success and the cost involved, I just stopped him. 'If you had any idea what this tooth has put me through, and the bad timing it was, you wouldn't even ask. I want revenge: take the fucker out altogether.' He laughed heartily and said 'OK, you're the boss, but this may hurt a little.' This may appear a strange thing to say, but going home minus the troublesome tooth to re-read newspaper reports of my success and bask in the local accolades, was sheer heaven.

The feeling didn't get to last long. Shortly afterwards my cousin, James Healy, suffered severe head injuries from a fall off a shed roof. He lived with his mother at home and he was all she had. Nanny was a typical old-fashioned woman, with a heart of gold, always friendly, and proud of her son. She had a deep faith and was incredibly strong. James was sent to Beaumont hospital and put on a life-support machine after operations failed.

I went to see him in hospital, a visit I will not forget until my dying day. I walked into that room and Nanny rushed over to me as if I was some kind of messiah with the power to change everything. She cried and pleaded, telling me James had been carrying a cut-out of the piece in the *Longford Leader* written about me – he was showing it to anyone who hadn't seen it, and still had the article in his pocket. I felt utterly and completely helpless beside her. I went from being on top of the world, ready for anything, to feeling hopelessly naked. Here was a situation that I could do absolutely nothing to influence. I never felt so utterly devastated. After several days, the difficult decision was taken to turn off the machine and let James go peacefully. My heart broke for Nanny. In truth, all this political stuff paled into insignificance at a time like this.

9

THE LIFE OF AN ÁRD COMHAIRLE MEMBER

The national executive of Fianna Fáil is a strange yet wonderful institution. In theory, everything about it is noble and honourable. In theory, it is the perfect body to keep a party connected and well informed, and to give those at the top an opportunity to meet and discuss issues with the ordinary people. A perfect sounding-board for ideas of all kinds, in theory. I often thought that if a political party was being established today and you hired management consultants to organise it, they would probably come up with exactly this format too. However, that's all in theory. Practice, like everything else, is an entirely different matter.

Many hours have been wasted talking about reforming the national executive, but they usually come to very little because it's not that it needs reform – the ideas behind it are excellent – it's that it needs more participation, belief and use. And in truth that's never going to happen.

It was decided recently to make the Committee of Fifteen a Committee of Twenty, combining it with what used to be the women's group representatives. But what real difference this will make is very much open to question. First of all, you have the constituency and county representatives, one from every constituency – or, where two counties make up one constituency, one rep from each county is selected. This should allow all the top brass in each constituency to have a voice and to feed local concerns into the Party leadership. Wonderful idea. The problem is, constituency reps are usually 'lifers' and many of them don't provide anywhere near enough feedback to their local machines. But, then, they are not given the responsibility to do so; it is usually felt that they should just be thankful to sit alongside the great and the good of the national party once a month. There is no mechanism for them to feed their concerns into these meetings. The agendas are limited, rarely touch on national issues, and unless you jump up and try to stick your oar in, you may never get a chance to say anything. And, by God, there are plenty who are willing to get to their feet. Just when we all thought we were about to hit the pub, someone jumps up to give their perspective on East Timor! Another bloody spiel. It would be all right if we were going to debate the issue, but what's the point? It's not like anyone is listening at that stage. Take your free drink voucher and get to the Dáil bar quick!

The Committee of Fifteen was supposed to ensure that the lowest level of the organisation, the cumann, could elect fifteen people directly to the national executive, yet I never once heard a proposal brought forward on behalf of a local cumann. To be fair to the Party leadership, it is a vicious circle. They tend to treat the executive like monkeys, so the executive loses interest and starts to act like monkeys. That's fine so long as the monkeys eat the banana and are happy, but it doesn't serve the Party. From time to time a monkey fires a banana skin back at the table and then we have a bit of sport! But the more the Party leadership sees the executive acting up, the less they are willing to trust its members and the less information or involvement they are willing to grant them. So everyone starts to act the monkey all over.

Part of the problem is that the style of government has changed. Fianna Fáil is not the old parochial organisation it once was. It is slick and professional these days. Sure, Dev may have needed to talk to these kinds of people, but where else was he going to get advice? Today's ministers and leaders have a host of 'experts' and advisers on a whole range of topics, and a whole civil service to rely on also. I'm not criticising that system, it's very much necessary in a modern government, but I do think it a shame that it has to be at the expense of the old Party machinery. Once in a while many ministers could learn a lot by going to the national executive and asking their advice on an issue – if nothing else it would give them a sense of what Joe Public is saying. But the truth is that a minister would be laughed at if he proposed discussing government policy with the ordinary Party folk, and as a result he can often lose sight of what ordinary people think.

Ministers and HQ can't trust the executive to keep their gobs shut; that's another problem. They can't trust them to take responsibility for unpopular decisions with their own organisations back home. They can't trust them either to leave personal and petty gripes aside and think of the bigger picture. So the best that can be done is present them with a fait accompli. Work everything out in a subcommittee, then just run over the fancy bits at the executive, where policy can be rubber-stamped. The members of the executive, for their part, know they aren't trusted – even the media often has better information than executive members on what is happening in the Party. Most major decisions are made behind the scenes, so why should executive members take the heat in their local organisations or responsibility for decisions which weren't theirs to begin with?

I remember going to the executive for the first time. I was quite simply thrilled. This was it, my chance to stride across the national stage at Party level, winning access and respect. Part of something that had shaped Fianna Fáil since the very beginning. I got a wonderful welcome, handshakes that left my knuckles bruised. Geraldine Feeney giving me a big kiss. The meeting applauded, acknowledging me as the youngest of the Committee of Fifteen. Yes, these people knew how hard it was and recognised my achievement. And for me, sitting in between the Mayo and Donegal mafias – man, this was living!

The first thing I spoke on was Sunday working hours and protecting workers. I was nervous as hell, standing up in the Fianna Fáil party rooms, Dev, Lemass, Haughey and Reynolds all staring down at me from the walls, the famous newspaper cuttings screaming history, and Bertie Ahern waiting for me to speak as intently as Boris Yeltsin used to wait for his vodka to be opened. I loved it. They applauded. To be honest, no one gave a shite what I said, it was the fact that it was the first thing I said and I said it well. They wanted me to succeed. Christ, I couldn't get to sleep for two weeks after with the thrill of it! Such is life when you are a young politico. Anyone ever involved at a similar level in their own political party, whatever it may be, knows exactly what I am talking about.

After a good executive meeting, a group of us would head over to Buswell's. Kevin McGuinness, Damien Murphy, Peter Kelly, who was soon to be a TD, Timmy Dooley and Geraldine Feeney, who later became senators, a legendary constituency rep called Podge from Kerry, Dara Calleary, Iarla Duffy, John Watson. You could network for hours. The great and the good from across the country downing pints like a ministerial Merc guzzles petrol. Renard's usually followed, and that was usually followed by a very sore head the next morning, as well as a very wounded ego when I discovered for the umpteenth time that girls really didn't give a toss if I was on the Fianna Fáil national executive. Jaysus, take me back to Blazers in Longford, where I'll get some respect.

The great thing about the executive was the contacts it brought. Everyone got to know you. Ministers and TDs called you by your first name. Party HQ knew who you were. Martin Mackin was general secretary at the time, and he was always willing to stand and chat or have a drink with you at one function or another. And you were asked to everything, from cumann meetings to gala receptions in Dublin Castle. At the time Dun Laoghaire Ógra Fianna Fáil were very active and organised some great events, and in general they were a very nice crowd. There were more than a few romantic encounters in this social scene, but no one ever showed much interest in me. Funny that.

Over at Trinity College, Avril Power and a very strong group of students had managed to wrest control of this old bastion away from the left-wing pinkos. Avril was incredible in her work rate and her political talent, and the main thing was that she stood up for her party no matter who tried to knock it or how difficult the issue in question might have been. Mary Hanafin made a very wise decision in appointing her as an adviser when she became minister.

But the TCD cumann also organised some wonderful nights – quizzes, lectures; you name it, they were doing it. I always enjoyed them, even though I must admit that I found the TCD atmosphere intimidating. I mean, let's face it, I was a country boy through and through. My alma mater (as university heads would call their former college) was Dundalk RTC, which never had any airs or graces. I just didn't 'get' the university thing. There was always a look of disdain at the fact that you didn't have a degree and weren't studying, and of course your political views were too parochial. Mind you, the TCD Fianna Fáil people were great. I guess they respected you for different reasons, but the reception outside of that was never something I took to.

I apologise to all the nice TCD people out there; it's just my view, and like I always say, you don't have to agree with it. To others, I don't mind telling them to get their head out of their arse lively. Or, given some of the political opinions in the college, maybe that is the best place they could keep it.

Kevin Barry Cumann (KBC) in UCD did invite me out once to a function but I was going on holidays at the time and couldn't make it. Later on I got an opportunity to compare UCD with TCD, but I'm getting way ahead of myself at this point. Besides I was never an expert in Ógra, it was far too complex for me. But people who knew Ógra had already terrified me with stories of bloodletting in KBC in the past, when, apparently, even talking to the wrong person could get you thoroughly shafted and your name would be muck overnight.

I hated the Party's youth wing, to be honest. The senior party was the place for me. I loved the old political dogs at cumann meetings, the banter, the sheer hatred of the opposition, the siege mentality. These people cared about the Party above everything and going to functions and parties and meetings was just part of the adventure. The truth was that they could buy and sell most of the younger Party members – and a large proportion of the supposed political experts in the country.

Every so often I would receive an invitation to a state event. It was the one small reward for doing a job that often involved a lot of expense but which paid absolutely nothing, and your expenses were your own problem. I remember being at a function in Dublin Castle one night, and as myself and Kevin McGuinness sauntered around among the assembled guests in St Patrick's Hall, gazing up at the ornate ceiling and sipping a very agreeable wine, he turned to me and said, 'Jaysus, Johnny, just think of all the men who died so a couple of upstarts like us could be here tonight.' It was a joke, of course, but a very sobering thought all the same. While they may not have died for us in particular, it was true that we were here, members of a big nationalist political movement, sipping wine in what used to be the seat of British power in Ireland. God bless Dev!

I thought, too, of the many men and women I knew in Fianna Fáil who were old now and had spent a lifetime supporting the Party without ever getting so much as this free glass of wine. So I topped up my glass and thought, this one's for them! I don't remember getting home that night, but I did wake up in the digs with my head on the bed and my legs still lying on the floor, and I was late for work.

Throughout 1999, things were looking good for Johnny Fallon. I was settling in to my new job in Ryan Glennon. They had a great crew of people there at the time. Daragh Brehon from Limerick seemed to be fascinated by my political adventures, Mick McElligott from Kerry was just bemused by them, but that was his nature! Anthony Hanniffy was from Offaly, and you always knew you were OK with people from Laois–Offaly. Ah, the heartlands.

The local elections were coming up, and a lot of people were talking about me at the time, a lot of people were saying I would run. The problem was, no one was talking to me. People tended to forget that I was still only twenty-two, and I needed advice and encouragement. Maybe that in itself was proof that I was still too young. I thought long and hard about it, and I knew I wanted it. Yes, I was working in Dublin, but I was home every weekend and with meetings and other commitments I was often home midweek as well. In fact, I was clocking up over 25,000 miles a year in my old 1991 Nissan Sunny. Due to the support I had from my family, I knew it was feasible for me to have an office and hold regular clinics, things I knew no other candidate would provide. I had also experience from other parts of the country, where information and newsletters were a key success factor, but unheard of where I came from. However, I had a view about these things. OK, here comes the science bit.

My local electoral area was Ballymahon. It had six seats: three Fianna Fáil and three Fine Gael. One FF councillor, Paddy Farrell from my parish, was retiring. In the last election, in 1991, we had run three candidates and it had not gone well. John Nolan, who ran as an independent, was elected, though he later joined Fianna Fáil. This time the consensus was that we should run three or four candidates, depending on the geography. It was my view that I sat perfectly between the parishes of Cashel and Rathcline. I felt we should run one candidate between the two parishes, and of course that should be me. Alternatively, I would be happy to run in Cashel as part of a four-man team, provided we worked closely on transfers with the Lanesboro candidate.

I approached Cashel cumann secretary Pat Cunningham, and to be fair he didn't say much either one way or the other, but I must admit I was disappointed. It was the first time I hadn't received unqualified support from the word go. I decided that, while I wanted the nomination, I was not going to do what I saw too many others do, and divide the Party at convention before we ever got going. Whatever happened, it would be decided before the convention was held. That was probably a mistake. My father contended that if I went before convention in Ballymahon, the chances were I would win, as I was very popular among many of the cumainn at the time.

Eventually my father suggested to both Cashel and Lanesboro cumainn that they meet with Fermoyle and clear things up. While everyone agreed this was a good idea, no one seemed to want to follow it through, and it didn't come to anything. It was clear to me that, with the departure of Paddy Farrell as a sitting councillor, Lanesboro was determined to have a candidate in that area, and that probably made a certain amount of sense too, to be fair. I understood the message that I was getting: if there was one candidate, Johnny Fallon would be it, but we want our own candidates and therefore Johnny Fallon must be kept out of the equation.

I decided to talk to Peter Kelly, who would later become a TD. He looked at me and said, 'Listen, would you win a seat? Tell me now, do you think you can do it?' My answer was an emphatic yes. To which he replied, 'Then get your arse back out there and sit down with these guys and make them see it your way.' But that was easy for him to say. Lanesboro already had Pat Sullivan, a retired schoolteacher of impeccable Party standing, lined up, and Cashel had John Kenny, who was also a young candidate, being only in his thirties at the time. So I decided to talk to the secretary of the comhairle Dáil ceanntair, Tom Donlon, who in general was the Party fixer in Longford and would be talking to everyone about the possibilities. Tom just said to me plain and simple, 'You have a great future ahead of you, and you are certain to go to the very top some day, but this is not your battle, you're still just that bit too young. Hang on and your time will come.' I respected Tom's opinion enough to think long and hard about his advice.

I spoke to John Kenny several times, too, and he was the one person who really wanted me to do it. He said that he would gladly support me, but I knew he was under pressure from others to run himself. John was a great guy who without doubt would think of the Party ahead of himself. When Cashel cumann finally called a meeting to decide on a candidate, I was invited, though there was never a suggestion that they were going to support my candidature. John Kenny was proposed and seconded and everyone spoke extremely highly of him and rightly so. I suppose part of me was hoping someone would mention my name, but no one did. Finally I stood up to congratulate John, and with every ounce of Fianna Fáil blood that was coursing through my veins, I made it clear that we should be united at convention and I wouldn't stand against John Kenny. I meant it too. Our constituency had been ravaged with silly divisions before, and I was not going to add to that now.

Lanesboro later selected Pat Sullivan, and I also offered him my support. I consoled myself with the thought that the Party should be able to hold on to its three seats, with Barney Steele and John Nolan as sitting councillors and John Kenny or Pat Sullivan helping each other to the last seat. However, things started to go wrong at convention. The boundaries had been re-drawn, putting Ardagh in with the Ballymahon area, and as they had a sizeable pocket of votes they wanted to put forward a candidate too. I thought they were too close to the leading Fine Gael light, James Bannon, who had a huge vote in the area, but I will come back to this point later.

A row ensued and there were several murmurs of people running as independents. I was sickened by it, especially since I had not pushed things in my own area just to avoid such conflict. Eventually, to avoid having an independent, the convention agreed to run five candidates for three seats. In hindsight, it can only be described as a foolish and stupid mistake. I voted to allow all five to run, but that was to stop the row, and like many others I knew in my heart it was the wrong strategy. Even the local media were astounded by the decision.

At the next meeting I made another mistake. I was proposed as Director of Elections for the area, and, naively, I believed the hype that surrounded me since my success on the national executive. They talked me up and I accepted the position, in the end running a campaign I didn't agree with in terms of the numbers or the geography, and a group of candidates who were never likely to be able to pull together, such was the scrapping for votes. I wanted them to face the electorate as a team, but found out early on that no one was really canvassing for No. 2 votes for other Fianna Fáil candidates on the doorsteps. They distrusted each other. I wanted them to push home the point that there was no use in just electing one Fianna Fáil councillor for their own area, that a councillor needed support and people needed to vote for the Fianna Fáil team. No candidate took up this challenge. I wanted candidates who shared areas to bring out joint literature on their proposals, emphasising the need for vote transfers. But this was also a fantasy.

The only proposal I succeeded in laying down was to divide the areas for the first weeks of the campaign. I got an ordnance survey map and the electoral registers of every polling booth. I went down to Quinn's in Drumcondra on a quiet afternoon and took up an entire corner of the pub sorting through the maps and registers, calculating and recalculating. Two young students approached me and sat down for a chat, thinking I was into surveying or engineering, and when they found out what I was doing they decided I was pretty boring. A man who supported the Socialist Workers Party called me all the names under the sun, until I bought him a drink, told him I loved Fianna Fáil and always would, so he shrugged and said, 'Ah, I suppose you're not all bad.'

So I sat in Quinn's and looked at what candidate was nearest and most likely to get the votes from the next, how many people were involved, and I tried to give a similar proportion of the electorate to each candidate. In the end, John Kenny had the least with just over 1,200 voters, and Barney Steele the most with almost 1,500. I met the candidates later on and made my thinking clear: there were too many of them, they would do each other more harm than good, and the areas I had outlined were their protection. I pointed out in my old-school way that any Fianna Fáil candidate should be able to poll 33 per cent of the vote in any given location, and the general election results from booths backed me up on this. I told each candidate to look at the total of voters I had given them, and if he could come back to me on election day with 33 per cent of the vote in his own area, that would be at least 400 first-preference votes and he would have a damn good shot at getting elected.

Of course, the common wisdom in local elections is that, because the areas are so small and local factors such as family have such a big part to play, candidates must be allowed a so-called 'free-for-all period', when they can canvass wherever they like. If I had my way again I wouldn't have let them have this, simply because I never felt they concentrated enough on the home villages and were too interested in pulling votes from elsewhere. We had too many candidates for any kind of free-for-all period anyway. Then again, if I had my way I would never have taken up the position in the first place.

One candidate approached me and asked could he move into other areas before the given embargo was up. I refused. He looked at me and said, 'But I have my area done and people are looking at me and asking, "Why are you coming around again? Do you not trust us?"' If I had been him, my answer would have been, 'No, I don't, I want to make sure.' You can never, ever do too much work in your home territory in an election.

During the campaign, my methods of electioneering upset many people in Ardagh. They were of the view that their candidate, Pat Farrell, who was a very able guy and should have been a strong candidate, could pick up a lot of James Bannon's No. 2 votes. Therefore they did not want to attack Fine Gael too hard. As Director of Elections, it was my job to look after the entire field, and that could not be done by pussy-footing around the Blueshirts. I have never subscribed to the theory that you can pick up second preferences that way. No matter how nice a Fine Gael candidate is, they won't get my No. 2 over a Fianna Fáil man. I have always believed that people will vote according to who they think will do the job, who is strong, who will speak up for them and who will lead them. Floating voters who vote Fine Gael No. 1 will be more likely to vote No. 2 for another strong candidate, rather than someone who is afraid of the main player. I also knew that, because we had too many candidates, No. 2 votes were worth fuck-all. We needed people's No. 1. What's more, we needed people to continue their preference right down through the Fianna Fáil candidates.

I failed miserably in getting that message across to the candidates. I made a hard-hitting speech in Ardagh and everyone was in uproar afterwards, but at that stage of the campaign I think I already knew we were in trouble and I was fed-up watching on. I lashed out, and to be honest I would do the same again. People never won elections by being timid. It's as simple as that. I kept talking up our chances to everyone but I was admitting privately that we had already lost. There was no shape, direction or structure anymore and I didn't feel I had control of the candidates. Except for Barney Steele, who was a model candidate. I never had to speak to him. He was only interested in his home area and he tried to play his part in everything I suggested. It wasn't surprising he topped the poll for Fianna Fáil.

I sat one night with the two assistant directors of elections, John Browne and Mick Cahill, and we all bemoaned the fact that we had far too many in the field. Mick turned to me and said, 'I thought you were sure to run out in your county, and we would only have had one there then.'

'Yeah, sure why didn't ya?' John Browne added. 'Aren't you the perfect man for it there, and you'd be better placed to have a bearing on this then.'

'It would have solved an awful lot of the problems,' Mick remarked.

'Ah, who knows?' I said. 'Maybe it would have caused a hundred more.'

John Kenny ran a hard campaign. He was always up against it, with such a small electoral base and a veteran of two previous elections, Seán Farrell, opposing him. John tried his best to do the right thing. He tried to listen and work but as the campaign got scrappier he found everyone eating into him, including his fellow Party candidates, and he just couldn't get the vote out. Pat Sullivan gave it his all but his campaign was too isolated from the others. And he suffered from an ageist thing, with people saying he was too old to start out as a councillor now, an unfair accusation, in my view, because age should never come into such an equation; ability is all that matters. Pat was running against a sitting Fine Gael councillor, Adie Farrell, and he failed to make any significant impact on his first-preference vote.

John Nolan held his seat, but only just. His rivalry with Pat Farrell in Ardagh had been the greatest bone of contention; they both struggled to get a solid first preference and, disappointingly, Pat Farrell made absolutely no impact on James Bannon's first preference in that side of the constituency. This sounded the death knell for the Fianna Fáil team. I remembered the words of Abraham Lincoln when he lost an election: 'Like a boy who stubs his toe in the dark, too old to cry, but hurt too much to laugh.'

At the next comhairle ceanntair meeting I gave my views, complimented the candidates and took the responsibility for our failure at the polls. Pat Sullivan came up to me and said, 'Ah, sure it can't be helped. These things happen. You need to get yourself a woman and forget all this running about.' His wife, meanwhile, confided to my mother that they had been waiting to see if I would announce my candidacy, and when they heard nothing from me they thought that Pat would go for it, but that they felt I would have been a strong candidate. It was cold comfort at this point.

I was fairly fed up with things at that stage. Nothing seemed to fit right and I was far from happy. Albert was still a TD but had clearly left the stage and the edge was gone from politics. A lot of people I considered friends were getting on a bit and taking a back seat. Others, like Tony Farrell, tragically, had passed on. For some reason I wasn't getting the same buzz out of it. Maybe too many of the old team were moving on, for my liking, or maybe I was fed-up with it interfering in my life. I knew things desperately needed a change. I was getting tired of hitting Blazers every weekend, seeing the same people, meeting the same girls, going nowhere and never being any closer to feeling that my life was getting sorted out.

Although I was enjoying the national executive, I was beginning to look at my finances and wondering, now that I had made my contacts, if I should really bother running again. But enough people were convincing me that I should go for it, even though my success had clearly brought a flood of new candidates out of the woodwork and it was going to be a much more crowded field next time.

So there you are, motoring along with your humdrum life, sick of Dublin, work was OK but far from the dream job, fed up with Blazers on a Saturday night, and McGowan's all through the week – not that that ever stops you going, mind. Then one day when you have almost given up and are tired of thinking of all your missed opportunities, everything changes. And I mean everything.

When my sister announced her engagement to Kenneth Rollins we were all delighted, and to celebrate this momentous occasion we were all going to head to the Peer Inn for a right good piss-up. On the day, Margarita asked me to go to Ballymahon and meet two of her friends from college so as I could show them the way to our house through the maze of roads. I was not too happy having to go; I was quite content sitting in my room playing the guitar. I drove up and saw them parked outside Finnegan's garage on Main Street, and as I turned the car, the girl in the passenger got out. I was glad I was the one meeting them all of a sudden. So I led the way on the journey back, and took full measure of this girl, Annette. Not that she seemed to pay me much heed, mind you. So I went to the bathroom, brushed the old teeth and gelled the hair, dug out my latest purchases from Spirit Fashions on Dublin Street where all hip young Longford men shop if they want to score, and got myself ready for the night.

Margarita's other friend, Rose, sat between Annette and me, and although she was all chat it was Annette I wanted to talk to. Rose asked me about politics and the national executive, but at this stage I was tired talking about it to people as it usually led to my being asked to do something. I was holding clinics with people as often as some councillors, even when there was precious little I could do in many cases. But I digress. Annette walked up to the bar and I sat watching her cross the floor. I very nearly broke my jaw when it hit the ground as I saw that sexy ass pass by me. Oh, Lord, help me!

For some reason everyone kept buying me pints because I was the brother of the bride to be, and I couldn't keep up with them all. I was well plastered by going-home time. When we got back to the house, I treated Annette, this sophisticated city girl, to the pleasure of me dancing around the kitchen singing, 'If you wanna be my lover, you gotta get with my friends,' and to my many theories on threesomes. Smooth as ice cream me. Anyway, whether it was my singing or just the late hour, we ended up alone, and I decided that it was time to make a move. She didn't object, and being used to having to wrestle a girl for some time before finally getting to kiss her, I did find this unusual, but I just thanked God for alcohol.

Amazingly, she gave me her phone number, and I told her I would call when I got back to Dublin. I knew she had no idea what she was getting herself into, and I saw no reason to make her any the wiser. As this was Sunday, I decided to play things very cool and I didn't ring her until Monday.

When we met up again the following Wednesday she was sick with a throat infection. She told me, 'Oh, that's something you should know about me, I'm always sick.' I laughed at the time but, as you will see, she wasn't bloody messing. She didn't want to kiss me in case she gave me the infection, but, I mean, do you really think I cared about an infection? I wanted kissing, more kissing. 'There, there, shut up about infections'.

Everyone at work laughed when I told them we were meeting again the following Friday, 'Johnny, Johnny, have you never heard of overkill?' Well, I didn't care, I wanted to see her as much as possible before she discovered that she didn't like me. By the time the Friday date was over, though, I knew I was in trouble. I was totally smitten, in love.

I left my car in Trinity College, and by the time we left the pub the gates were locked. Annette tried to climb the railings to get in because I had left the inside light on, and all I could think of was 'Wow, what a girl, only a Dub would do that for you and risk getting arrested.' I convinced her to come back down, and we walked around the back to Kennedy's pub where the bouncers very kindly let us onto the Trinity grounds so as I could at least switch off the car lights. Luckily, when we got in we found a groundskeeper heading for the gates and he let us get the car out.

Annette's birthday was on 4 December and mine just six days later, so we were both in line for presents galore. I brought her to Boulevard Café, a restaurant with good Longford connections, and we had a great meal and the most perfect of nights. By Christmas, we were talking about saving to get a place together. Yes, it really happened that quickly. I had spent so long being unsure that when it finally happened I was in no doubt that this girl was everything and I was just crazy about her. Her roots were Fianna Fáil but she wasn't into politics. She had known people in Fine Gael and knew Paul Gogarty of the Green Party but that was about it. But she and I could talk for hours about stuff, and I was so proud when after a couple of months of dating she said to me, 'You know, for all the other people I've known in politics, I never cared for it. You are the first person involved in Fianna Fáil that I've met, and for the first time I can really see politics working, really making a difference.' So, while all of you Fianna Fáil haters out there will scoff at that, the simple fact is we do the work and that's why we are still No. 1.

When the executive elections came around in early 2000 I found it hard to gather the same energy. I was late deciding that I was definitely going, and to be fair to the Longford machine, after the locals they wanted a rest and it was hard to motivate everyone to the same level so soon again. I had a candidate on my doorstep in Westmeath, another candidate much younger than me in south Kildare, and then Gearóid Lohan, who had a huge vote from his Galway base, switched constituencies to Leinster. John Watson wasn't running in Donegal so I lost a voting agreement there, and the Connacht field near my Longford base was also crowded. Everyone was of the same opinion: Johnny Fallon was the one to beat in Leinster. I was going to get very few people voting for me who wanted someone else in Leinster; they had to keep my vote down. And of course I suffered that age-old problem, 'Ah, sure, Johnny is fine, he doesn't need the votes. He'll fly in.'

Donie Cassidy was also lost to me, due to there being a West-Meath candidate. I was being squeezed on all sides and it took all the ability and ingenuity of the Longford machine to get any kind of vote at all outside of our own sixty-six.

Annette canvassed for me, and found it a tough experience. She wasn't impressed if people walked away and threw my flyer in the bin, or if she saw a flyer of mine on the ground and people walking on it. Hey, she loved me! One man stopped when she asked him for a vote for me and he said, 'And who are you, now?'

'I'm his girlfriend,' Annette replied.

He held her by the arm, looked her in the eye and said, 'Oh, dear love, you are in for a long and difficult road.'

The reaction was good in general, name recognition was high, and at least no one had anything bad to say about me. Donie Cassidy and my Dad thought it would be close. I had an idea that my base was too small for such a crowded field, and in the end I was right, but it was a close thing. The Longford machine had pulled off an amazing achievement in helping me to poll 1,240 votes – another 40 would have seen me retain the seat. They don't come much closer than that.

10

MOVING ON

You might think that I would be gutted, but it didn't really bother me at all, I could take or leave it at this stage. I knew I had made the contacts I needed.

Annette was more disappointed than me, and blamed herself a bit, but the truth was that not sitting on the national executive was irrelevant because no one really cared whether I was there or not. The experience had taught me that much, at least. Anyway, I was much happier finally feeling like I had a career and a girlfriend and a supportive family back home, and these were more important than anything else. I was tired of trying to keep people happy politically.

The local papers were all talk about who would succeed Albert, and when I threw my name in the ring the *Longford Leader* ran an article. I even made it into *The Irish Times* and the *Sunday Tribune*. I never actually thought I could defeat either Councillor Peter Kelly or Councillor Denis Glennon in a contest but I reckoned I could at least lay down a marker, rattle things up a bit, after all that's what I'm best at. And I always loved long odds. I never really did much by way of campaigning for nomination to run as the Longford candidate however, and I had my own idea for how it would progress if it were to happen, and that was that I didn't want to draw attention early on. Better if I started by getting cumann support and then making a dash at the end. Anyway, the election wasn't until 2002 and we were talking about early 2000 at this stage. It was a lifetime away.

It's never as easy as simply deciding that you want to run for election. If you do want to stand, you need to consult with your cumann and win their backing. After that, you have to prepare for convention, where all the cumainn have votes. Winning this is not easy. A lot depends on geography, experience and political ingenuity, and people's belief in who can go furthest in the job. Conventions are notorious for causing problems; getting selected can sometimes be every bit as hard as getting elected. When Longford and Roscommon were first put together as a constituency in 1992, we held the convention in the hall in Ballyleague with Pádraig Flynn as chairman. We went in at 8 p.m. and the Longford delegates selected Albert as the only candidate in the county, so half an hour later our work was done. Roscommon delegates were still selecting their candidates at 5 a.m. the following morning. I was sent out just after midnight with my mother to bring back chips and burgers for everyone, including the great P. Flynn.

When it came to winning support within the Party, I knew there was no doubt but that Ógra would back Peter Kelly. He had fostered it, supported it, helped it grow. He deserved their support. But I think both Dennis Glennon, who taught many of the Ógra lads in school, and myself as a former member, thought that, while they would give Kelly the vote, they would at least give us the opportunity to speak to Ógra's membership. We could at least get the chance to demonstrate our ability, even if Ógra as a unit didn't back us. When the *Longford Leader* carried an article on potential candidates, Ógra said that they would support Peter Kelly and that was that, no matter who else ran. It was a typical Ógra error. There was absolutely no need to announce who you were voting for that far in advance of a convention. Other candidates had been given no opportunity to talk with members. It didn't help Peter Kelly either. He was glad of the votes, but Ógra's move made it look somewhat underhand, even though Peter had never put any pressure on the youth wing at all.

And if Ógra wasn't backing the young candidate, that was damaging to me. I knew they would owe it to Peter but I didn't expect to have to deal with that question so long before a convention was even held. I was well pissed off. So were some Ógra members, who apologised to me, and much later many of them couldn't look Dennis in the eye at convention. The stupid thing was there was no need for it, it was all easily avoidable by having patience and following procedure. To be fair to most of the Ógra committee, they had discussed the issue among themselves and they knew who they were going to vote for, and they simply didn't see any point in not revealing their decision. Perhaps they had a point, but it wouldn't have been my way of doing it.

So much back-biting was going on in the Party that it was very hard to listen to it all. I had other things to worry about in any case. Annette was sick again. After numerous bouts of the 'flu she then had gallstones, and as we didn't have health cover she had to go on a waiting list, all the time consuming painkillers like Smarties. We rang the hospital every day, and every day it had no bed. We brought her to A&E in Beaumont – Annette's GP said it was the only way as she was in such serious pain. We waited hours, only for a doctor to tell her it was a kidney infection, even though she had scans to prove she had acute gallstones. We felt that the delay in getting the operation was completely unacceptable, but none of our enquiries seemed to get us anywhere. Eventually, after I contacted the Ombudsman about the matter one Thursday morning, the hospital reverted to us at 6 pm that evening, having finally found a bed.

The crazy thing is that people blame ministers for this mess! Politicians' main problem is that they can't stop fighting with each other; if they did, and sat down for a minute and agreed a political approach across parties to take on vested interests and ridiculous work practices, they could probably sort out the mess that is our health system. Instead, every minister of every party becomes another victim of a system which no one politician can control without massive public and political support.

I wasn't well myself and actually had a cancer scare during the year. It turned out to be nothing, but the episode made me wonder what the hell I was doing. When an opportunity came up to move jobs once again, this time to the finance department of A&L Goodbody, the biggest law firm in the country, I jumped at the chance. It meant more money and more opportunity. Another attempt to get the old career in shape.

I met with the Cashel cumann to discuss my running for the seat in Longford. I laid out why I thought it was feasible and then put it to them that I would only run with their backing. I knew other cumainn like Fermoyle would nominate and support me but I wanted Cashel as my home parish. I put them in an awkward position because I effectively asked them to declare their support for me there and then, but I knew that if I was to have any chance that had to happen for me now, and if they didn't go with it at least I knew where I stood. I looked on it as a win–win situation. I went outside to allow them deliberate, and waited with Annette in the car. When I went back they told me that they felt the time wasn't right for me to go for it, I was still a bit young. They did, however, say that I definitely was TD material. I had all the cut and style of a politician, the knowledge and the support, and that if I just bided my time a little longer it would all fall into place because it just had to at some stage for someone like me. I'll always have those words with me in my head. It's nice to refer to them and think that at least one group of people thinks that of me.

For all the nice words, though, that was the end of me running for TD. It came down to a number of factors. Firstly, I had a life now. I was settling into A&L Goodbody and I really liked the atmosphere of the company in general. The department was mostly female except for the bosses, Jim McSweeney and Des Murray, along with Keith Walsh and myself. Keith and I became good friends, being trapped as we were among so many women. We saw ourselves as the voices of reason.

But I wanted more from life than simply chasing politics, which is all I had ever done up to this point. I mean you have to admit that having read this far you can begin to see how my mind was thinking. Could you have allowed your life to revolve so totally around a political party? There was a definite danger of burn-out at this stage.

I enjoyed the journey back to Dublin in the car with Annette that night after the Cashel meeting. I no longer had those lonely drives on my own, she was always willing to tag along even to the most boring of meetings just to keep me company. I was glad to be able to talk to her about us doing things together and being a couple, rather than explaining how little time we would have together, had a campaign been on the way. I always thought I would have been heartbroken to be told I wasn't to run, after all I was born to run. I knew that. But at the same time it didn't really upset me, perhaps further proof that I truly wasn't quite ready for the job. You see, that's the thing you always have to trust in the judgement of the wise old cumann members, because while they may get the occasional thing wrong, their collective experience is usually right.

My father never ran for election because, as he said himself, he was 'too controversial'. What he meant was that he had a view and he believed in it. He would not be shaken in his belief, and left no room for diplomacy. If you were part of a group, whether GAA or politics or anything else, and you were in an argument, launching my father at your opposition was the equivalent of a nuclear missile strike. In other words, when all hell broke loose you called on Mike Joe. It will not be pretty when it is over, there will be a lot of people hurt and upset on all sides, but by God it will end it. Politicians by their nature aren't cut from that cloth; voters usually don't appreciate such a singular and forceful personality. Politicians must be diplomatic, they must try to appease many divergent groups and can rarely afford to alienate portions of the electorate. I picked up many of those skills from my mother, but I must admit that for the first time, now that I was free of the burden of having to prove myself as a candidate, I could see a lot of fun and freedom in my father's position. Sometimes I guess you have to be fearless of the consequences, and of what people might think of you, when you believe in something. It brings its own respect.

Annette's family were great and I got on wonderfully well with all of them. I got on really well with all her friends, too, which is always a big test for a guy to pass. We used to meet up with them every Saturday night in Kenny's in Lucan village, Annette, Anita,

Ash and Ash. I know you will wonder, after all my talk of Dubs and Dublin, how I managed to cope at all, but the truth was that it all fitted together nicely. Lucan is a very strange hybrid of a place. It is full of contradictions. It has a population the size of the entire county of Longford yet it is only a suburb. It has grown beyond all recognition in the last fifteen years. The fields where Annette used to play are now housing estates and motorways. The village is almost rural in its atmosphere, yet it is situated at the side of a motorway and suffers from severe congestion.

There are two kinds of people living there, old Lucan and new Lucan. Old Lucan people use the village, know a lot of their neighbours and are very proud of their parish. They are highly political, drink in their local and still hang around with mates of theirs from school. They feel under threat from the new Lucan people. The area they knew has changed completely and they fear that it is dying forever.

Then you have the new Lucan people. Many hardly even know that Lucan village exists or what kind of shops are in it – they prefer to nip up to Liffey valley even though traffic congestion is worse there. They rarely know anything about their neighbours except their first names, and drink with work colleagues in the city rather than the Lucan locals. The new Lucanians are transient and usually move again after five years or so, and they don't have a huge interest in parish affairs, often believing that being involved in parish work in the counties they hail from is far more important. They have little interest in the politics of the area. Those involved in the big parties remain involved in their home counties, while the others have their heads turned by the novelty of what are new parties to them, like the Greens and independent candidates.

I admit that, had I moved to Lucan and not been with Annette, I would have been a typical new Lucanian, but it was amazing seeing things from a different perspective. Now, don't get me wrong: I'm a culchie and the Dubs wreck my head, but Lucanians deserve something more. The 'true' Dubs consider them boggers, while the culchies see them as Dubs, leaving these poor unfortunates not knowing what the hell they really are at all. I have been so often in places like Portlaoise and Mullingar and listened at meetings to the locals complain, quite rightly, about people from Dublin moving in, commute to work in the city every day and give nothing to the community except to push up the price of houses. It is a serious problem, and Lucan is another place where a distinct and separate community has become seriously endangered by hordes of people moving in and bringing nothing to the community. That may sound harsh but, feck it, it needs to be said.

Considering the amount of country people living in Lucan, it would only make sense that there should be significant Fianna Fáil or Fine Gael voters among them, yet neither of the main parties can get a councillor, never mind a TD, elected here. Why? Oh, I know you are going to give me a lecture now on all the things that are wrong or right in the area and on the past and blah blah blah. That's not worth diddley squat and everyone in politics knows it. Lucan has many problems, but they are the same problems that have been encountered by suburbs of major cities the world over. While some would like to say that some form of underhand dealing made things worse, the truth is that West Dublin is the only direction left for the city to expand in. The problem is that in the rush to provide much needed housing, the infrastructure has not been put in place to deal with the growing population. It's an unfortunate effect. However while in an ideal world we would put infrastructure in place first, we all know deep down that the reality is that people cannot be left waiting for somewhere to live while this is being done. The only viable option is to try do things in stages and that is what the government and planning authorities have now proposed with the new Adamstown development, we can only hope that it will be a success. It is crucial to note though that what is needed is participation. Mainstream parties have long since realised that you cannot simply oppose all development and growth, it is a natural thing that has to happen. The best policy is to accept that roads must be built and new developments planned but you get to have some say in how these are done if you agree with the theory in the first instance. In Lucan the problem is that most representatives now are abstentionist, in other words they oppose all proposals and therefore feed nothing into their planning, this is an easy way to get votes and become popular but unfortunately the problems for people on the ground just keep getting worse and that is exactly what is happening in Lucan.

The Greens aren't successful in Lucan because of policies – they have never been in power to implement one single piece of policy for the benefit of the area. What's happened is that the two big parties have lost their machines. Like the old Lucan people, they feel swamped; they don't know people anymore. The cumainn are defunct and only held together by a couple of people worn out by the pace of change, too tired to keep up. Both Fianna Fáil and Fine Gael long for the old days. Meanwhile, new parties like the Greens and independent candidates feed off people's disaffection, and actively encourage a protest vote. The one thing I couldn't stand about Lucan was the politics. There were a lot of sensible people but they didn't bother to vote, and too much of what was said by smaller parties and independents was allowed go unchallenged by the major parties, who were just too jaded.

Peter Brady was a Fine Gael councillor in Lucan for many years. Now it's obvious that there is no love lost between me and the Blueshirts, but he lost his seat in 1999 in what was a precursor of Austin Currie, TD, losing out in 2002. Fine Gael lost these seats to the Greens and since then problems in Lucan have got worse and not better. Oh, but don't blame the Greens. 'What can we do about it?' They don't tell people that on the doorsteps! I have yet to hear a candidate making promises and then qualifying them by saying, 'Of course, if I'm not in government I will be totally powerless to influence anything.' Feck's sake, at least poor auld Peter Brady might try and there was some chance of him knowing someone with influence.

I used a Fine Gael example, because if I used a Fianna Fáil one you would surely accuse me of bias. That's the problem with being a Party man; it's too easy to dismiss my argument with a wave of the hand. Well, I will leave it to you, firm in my long-standing belief that history always proves me right.

I liked the Lucan folk. There was that old-fashioned culchie–Dubs banter, not the modern aggressive stuff but actual good-humoured slagging. The truth is, Lucan people are more like culchies than they care to admit, and have far more in common with country people than with some of their city neighbours. I settled in very well, the atmosphere was always good in the pubs, and I got to like the locals a lot. There you have it, I was finally beginning to settle into Dublin life, and I began to realise that it's all so much easier when you don't feel so alone.

Annette's friends used to ask me all the time why the culchies hate the Dubs so much. It's the kind of question you can never really answer satisfactorily. For most people it's the fact that Dubs and culchies have totally different viewpoints on things. It's not a one-way thing either, it's an age-old situation – city folk always look down on their country cousins as being less cool, fashionable and trendy than themselves. The ancient Romans did it to provincials. Londoners do it in England, Parisians in France. Don't you think that culchies get fed up of this? And, there you go, why are we called culchies? I mean, did we bother the Dubs so much that they had to think up a specific name for us? It speaks volumes that we don't have a name for them – we couldn't be arsed.

The enmity comes from the look a Dub will give you when you say you are into a particular band, as if you had no right to have even heard of them. It comes from when they look at you and say 'Oi'll fookin buuuuurst you, oi will', when all you are doing is standing at a bus stop. It's their dismissal of your humour and your experience as being somehow inferior to theirs. It's the lack of soul and community; the lack of a local. It's their abhorrence of Irish music and a bit of country as if listening to either will constipate them, even when they're full of shit already. It's their utter disregard for the bog, which is a vital part of Irish life. It's the fact that they are only interested in GAA so long as Dublin is playing. It's their refusal to walk any kind of distance at all; they need buses or trams to get anywhere. It's their teenage spawn, who have no respect for anything, and need to be dropped to school in case they might melt in the rain. It's the way the bus drivers are downright ignorant when you ask them about finding your way. It's the way they canoe down the Liffey. It's the way Dublin girls moan about what wasters the fellas are, but would never dream of dating a sound country man. It's the way Dublin men dress – fashion, my arse. It's the Dublin 4 over-educated, I-know-all-about-politics attitude. It's Dr Quirky's good time emporium. It's scangers. It's tracksuits. It's prices. It's the decent Dubs acceptance of scumbags in their midst. It's Pat Rabbitte. It's the fact that Dublin is a place where any auld rag tag can get elected – Greens, reds, socialists, communists; al Quaeda would probably get a few votes. Is that enough? No, I don't expect it makes any more sense to you now than when I began that little tirade. But it's a start.

Annette, however, had to get used to our strange country ways. And she did so admirably well. Especially things like 'late' closing in pubs. We went to Longford to celebrate the millennium and spent a great evening in the Peer Inn, not over-crowded – certainly not all hype and a high cover charge just to get in – with just Noel Carberry and Joe McGrath playing a few tunes and of course plenty of drink. Annette ended up stretched across the bar half-unconscious, for want of sleep more so than drink! Fr Mickey Murtagh asked me if she was all right, and I said of course and she jumped up and started yapping away. Next day she encountered him at mass, and at communion he gave her the host saying 'the body of Christ … Annette', just to prove he remembered her. She was mortified! Or, as they say in Dublin, 'scarlet'.

My sister finally married the love of her life, Kenneth Rollins, on 4 June 2000, and it was quite the occasion, with the reception in the Hodson Bay hotel. It wasn't helped by the fact that the diocese of Ardagh and Clonmacnoise has a rule that you can't get married on a Sunday. I can't understand it for the life of me. With the aid of some other priests in the diocese, we put her case to the bishop, but I was told that it was not possible because priests couldn't be expected to say Sunday mass and preside over a wedding on the same day! It galled me later in the year when I heard a priest attacking politicians for their lack of work. Apparently, our parish priest, a man my father had got on famously with up to that point, felt it would 'open the floodgates'. In a parish of a few hundred people and a church that would see maybe two or three weddings in a good year, I failed to understand this point.

Nevertheless, that was the date my sister wanted, so she ended up getting married in a church in Galway because they obviously have a different God down there who doesn't mind you getting married on a Sunday. Anyway, everything went swimmingly on the day, and Kenneth, the son of the man who used to run the little shop near by, and who had brought the news of my birth to my grandparents, was officially welcomed into the family!

It was funny, though. Growing up, it had always been my desire to stay local, to settle down at home and keep away from cities. Margarita had always had a far greater sense of adventure, but yet it was me who ended up working in the city and Margarita who settled down back home.

Political life was a lot easier for me at this point. There wasn't the same pressure, and although I would never have thought it, I found I really liked it that way. I kept up to speed, though. Longford Fianna Fáil held a kind of mini Árd Fheis, to call it that, and I was one of the speakers. I got a special compliment when junior minister Tom Kitt, who had to speak after me on the same subject, pulled me aside to pick my brains on a few topics because he 'hadn't had the chance to research them as well as you obviously had'. I was well impressed with my little self. I had a good chat on the day with Philip Reynolds also, Albert's son, who was still in the running for the seat. The amount of talk about who was going to take the seat was becoming ridiculous by now.

There are two schools of thought when it comes to conventions. One says you must have a convention early. This way a candidate has plenty of time to issue press releases, increase their profile and get known in the area. It is considered particularly beneficial when you have new candidates running. It is also said to allow for organisation and stability. On the other hand, there are those who believe in much later conventions. This way a candidate appears fresh and doesn't go stale, it allows less time for mistakes, and less opportunity for the opposition to get stuck into you. It's a bit like a manager delaying naming the team until just before kick-off. Of course, established candidates always prefer this anyway.

In reality, no one can claim to be an authority on this issue. Each constituency is different and what's good for one does not always work for another. However, although once upon a time I was a strong supporter of early conventions, I do think that the process has gone completely mad in the modern era. Except in exceptional circumstances, I think a run-in of six months should be enough for any candidate. A good candidate will build more than enough profile in that time. Announcing a candidate a year or more in advance robs them of news value, especially by the time of the vital election date, and also tends to make them look stale. I mean, let's face it, we all get tired of listening to some councillor or up and coming politico waxing lyrical in the local media week after week about the scourge of dog-shit on the pavement, just so they have something to say. Or, worse still, pontificating on fiscal rectitude and the delicate negotiations in Northern Ireland, as if they were a minister. I'm all for that in the final run-up to an election; in fact, it's very important that the electorate know how they handle those kind of issues. But what's the point at this stage, when to all intents and purposes they are still nobodies, two years away from even being an election hopeful! Give me a break! It also means that they end up talking about so many issues over that period of time that they end up having made a raft of promises at various meetings, most of which they can't even remember.

So, if you are an election hopeful, I will now dispense my golden nugget of wisdom. Candidates should have no more than three main areas that are a priority, and these they make promises on. Just three issues where they think they can deliver, and they should be fairly diverse and wide ranging. For the purposes of literature and debate, you should have what I call three more supplementaries. These are more visionary aims. They should relate to your three core aims but should not be promises. They are more a way of allowing people see what you want to lead them to, where you are going. They are objectives that you believe in but may not be attainable in the immediate future. Finally, whatever your core aims are, for God's sake believe in them. Never, ever make a promise or aim for something that your heart isn't 100 per cent behind. The electorate aren't fools. They can tell just from your voice whether or not you are committed to getting the result. If it isn't something you believe in, be big enough to say it. Don't lead the people on a merry dance and you will gain respect for it.

However, my views on conventions seem to be in a dying minority these days. Headquarters in all political parties are obsessed with getting conventions on and over as soon as possible. The fact is that many candidates, especially first timers, want it like that. It's a bit like Christmas: no one can wait to get their presents, and if there is a chance of bringing Christmas morning forward, everyone wants to see if Santa really did bring them what they asked for.

Either way, the Longford convention was to be held on 25 June 2001. Now you are probably wondering, if I wasn't going myself, surely I was getting behind someone else? Well, to be honest, not really. There were four people in the field. Philip Reynolds, whom I had known for a long time, and of course we were always a Reynolds family. Peter Kelly, who was a friend to our family for years, a mentor of mine and a major influence on me, a guy I will always respect and admire. Dennis Glennon, a former teacher of mine, an absolute gentleman, and someone who had similar views to mine on many issues. And finally Louie McIntyre, a councillor from Drumlish, who was a friend and supporter of mine whenever I needed it and whose sons I was also very good friends with. I truly was happy to see any of those get the nod. It's also true to say that my influence in the Party was now on the wane, my profile had dropped, and I knew people associated me with the old guard. Isn't that mad? I was old guard and not yet twenty-five!

I wasn't going to throw myself behind anyone but I also made it clear that if anyone asked for my help in any way they would get it, even licking stamps. I have never been one to question what task I'm given; just do what you are asked. Not surprisingly, they weren't knocking my door down on this occasion, when everyone wanted 'new' people in, and out with the old. The only one who did discuss their thoughts on running or who asked for any kind of assistance from me was Philip Reynolds. I suppose that was rather fitting; most people would have seen that camp as my natural home anyway. Maybe Philip felt that, if he was going for it, he needed the old Reynolds Guard more than the rest did. However, the problem was that Philip was running C&D pet foods in Longford, which is a major employer, and understandably it was difficult from a business perspective if the driving force behind it suddenly announces that he is leaving the position to fight an election. It creates uncertainty and is damaging to future growth, especially when the period of uncertainty is going to drag on for over a year and no one can be appointed in your stead for fear you don't succeed. The early convention certainly doesn't suit someone in that position.

I conveyed Philip's views and interests from time to time and got my head bitten off in a meeting of Ballymahon comhairle ceanntair for doing so. I lost the head a bit that night, but I was not going to accept from anyone an insinuation that I was playing a game or that it was all just 'bullshit' – in other words, lies. That type of accusation I take very seriously, and most people in Party meetings avoid such talk for that reason, but there are always some who still have a bit to learn. Of course, we all made up afterwards. In the end, Philip contacted me in early June to say that, having talked it over with all those close to him, he was not going to run. His first priority was his family and the business, and creating such uncertainty for the company could do serious damage for the future of both, which he was not prepared to do at that stage. I think he made the right decision.

Louie McEntire also withdrew, leaving just Glennon and Kelly. I expected Kelly to do it simply because I would be very surprised if a man of his experience was not able to work a convention and pull cumainn in behind him. Dennis Glennon was a good man and would have been a fine candidate, but he probably lacked the cold experience necessary at this stage. I managed to ensure that I did not have a vote at convention, as I did not want to choose between what were two very good friends. And with my head busted from all the talk and the way the whole thing exhausted the organisation, I booked a holiday to Egypt to coincide with the convention. A coward's way out? Perhaps, but I was fairly fed up being the strong and decisive character at this stage and I felt like just suiting myself.

Wandering among tombs, pyramids and temples is a fascinating way to take your mind off what might be happening at a convention back home. If the ancient sites aren't enough to distract you, the 45-degree heat, the hustlers continually looking for baksheesh, and the overpowering smell of camel shit certainly will. They are the things you never grasp from the movies. Egypt is an amazing country, but go see it quick. Considering that the police actively canvass you for money and will then let you climb a pyramid and take a lump of it, none of it may last all that much longer.

In any event, Peter Kelly won the convention. Dennis was gutted. I rang him when I got home to commiserate, and I could tell it had hurt him. These kinds of things always hurt us, even if we don't know why. I think the fact that several former students were marched into voting by Ógra, and seemed afraid to be seen chatting to Dennis, that hurt the most. It was a time when all of Ógra was being influenced by a sneaking respect for Sinn Féin methods, and wanted to run everything with military precision. Thankfully, I think that attitude is dying out, and there is a gradual acceptance that while Sinn Féin methods look attractive, they deliver feck-all seats by comparison with the tried and trusted way of Fianna Fáil.

I rang Peter to congratulate him and told him I was at his service for anything that I could do in the run-up to the election. I was delighted for him. If anyone truly deserved it, it was Peter. I would have walked across hot coals to get him elected if he asked.

So, all was well with the world. And it was to get better. I need-ed a new challenge in politics and it was about to come from a most unlikely source. I may have been taking a back seat in things, but I still had a myriad of contacts – friends, acquaintances, and the imprimatur of trust that service on the Fianna Fáil National Executive gives you. I mean that honestly. It applies even when you find yourself talking to someone in Fine Gael or the PDs or Labour. I had made many contacts in the other parties, and though they may have violently disagreed with my political views, they respected me for having a knowledge of politics. Naturally, I would always reciprocate that. Even at local level, Senator James Bannon knows that in an election I will go after him like the devil himself, with all the fury of hell ready to throw at him. I would show no mercy and I would expect the same from him. But I respect the man. I respect his knowledge and his position, and, once out of the Party fray, we could sit and chat and discuss what politicians or parties need to do without any rancour. While we might differ, there is always common ground, and I have found this to be the case with most people I know in politics. Politics is all about being free to attack all sides and people without fear, but also about being able to sit down like adults at the end of it all and make sense of things.

I had used the various contacts I had made to try and help people I knew from time to time, although not always successfully, but the odd time I did manage to do something for someone was a very rewarding experience. However, while sitting at my desk one day I got that message that's so familiar to all modern-day office workers, it flashed up on my screen: 'you have 1 new email message in your inbox'. I discovered it was a message to the entire firm, saying that A&L Goodbody were launching a new service called A&L Goodbody Consulting, and this would be headed up by Peter Brennan, who was joining the firm from IBEC. The consulting wing would focus on a number of areas, but one jumped out at me immediately: 'government affairs'. I felt one of those rare rushes of excitement. This was for me. I had no experience in the private sector of government business, but I was determined that I could fit in some how.

I wasn't a big enough fish to be able to march up to anyone in the firm and convince them I knew what I was talking about; after all, they knew nothing of my political past life. I figured I needed to find a way to get that across to Peter Brennan, preferably before he arrived. Since he was in IBEC, I needed an employer who might know him. Politics. Employer. Longford. Ringing any bells here, people? Yep, it was time to contact my old friend Philip Reynolds and ask him if he could pass on a quick reference about my political experience. He very kindly agreed to do so.

By the time Peter arrived in A&L he knew all about me, and because he is the kind of guy who is always willing to think outside the box, he was willing to trust me enough to help out with a project or two. Peter was unusual for a guy in his position; he was innovative and never afraid to try something new. I was already incredibly impressed by him and in no time was picking up all kinds of tips about how to work in this sector. He was well aware that what I had were raw political talents, and these just needed to be nurtured, tied down, smoothed out and adapted to suit a new purpose. I loved getting stuck into a project, even if I wasn't paid for it – after all, I had plenty of practice doing that for Fianna Fáil.

Meanwhile, I was still making the most of life with Annette. We were busy saving for a house, but the prices in Dublin were so crazy that it seemed an almost impossible dream. We were too well off for the council's shared-ownership scheme, but not earning enough for a mortgage. It wasn't like we had bad jobs; Annette was a full-time teacher. The fact is, we were in that lost category, and it really is disgraceful that there isn't some mechanism whereby private companies can provide a shared-ownership scheme similar to what the council does for low income households. This could be done by allowing the private investor tax relief for doing so, and could be a real election winner too. Should have kept that one to myself, actually.

I changed the car to a Rover 214, as the old Sunny had more than served its time – electioneering is very hard on a car. People slagged off Rovers, but it held the road like it was on rails, and was a really good drive, even if it was a bit slow on take off. My days of speed were far behind me now. I was a changed man. I was never in a rush anymore. I loved the anonymity of life. Annette, who had a masters in English literature, was a joy to listen to when she was talking about poetry or plays, or that other great passion in her life, Oscar Wilde. I was just grateful Oscar wasn't around anymore. Still, Annette would have to admit to being torn between his genius and my myriad abilities, such as being able to touch my nose with the underside of my top lip, or doing a dance where my legs went one way and my body the other (her friends all went crazy for that, don't ask why). I could even play the theme tune to Dallas by flicking my fingers against my Adam's apple. Yep, I'm the kind of guy you want at a party when a lot of drink has been consumed.

In 2001, Longford Town reached their first ever FAI cup final. What an occasion! It fitted so well with bright new Celtic tiger Ireland. The nothing team, the joke of the league for years, the club that might boast fifty people in Abbeycarton for a game not so long ago – how those of us who supported them had suffered! Nothing beats live football, the atmosphere and the craic at the ground. Television and big stars are all just bullshit. Sure, I supported Liverpool, but it was more of an interest than real support. I couldn't see them every week so I really couldn't feel the same way about them as I did about my local team. If Liverpool played Longford Town there was never any question as to who I was for. Nothing ever sickened me more than pre-season friendlies, when English teams would come over and total knob-ends would actually show up at the matches to cheer on the foreign side. Who are these sad gits? Like all League of Ireland fans, I support any Irish team in Europe no matter who they are playing. Then you have the gobshites who showed up to Ireland matches wearing Celtic jerseys! What is that all about? A Scottish team, staffed by eastern Europeans, whose only connection to Ireland is the fact that they sell their merchandise here, sing a couple of songs about the IRA, and have a four-leaf clover as a crest. Well, if that makes you Irish, then fuck me pink and call me the Queen. It galled me to hear so-called Celtic fans deride the League of Ireland and its players, while under some strange illusion that supporting Celtic makes them somehow more Irish.

Anyway, like a lot of women, Annette hates football. She might watch the odd Ireland match out of patriotism but that's about it. She hates to see it on television and can't imagine a more boring evening than being stuck watching it. She is not a big sports fan at all, in fact. However, when Longford played Bohemians in the final in Tolka Park, I eventually convinced her to try it. Two friends, Graham and Mark, who were Bohs fans, came along too.

The final fell on a great sunny day. We met up with the lads and headed into Drumcondra, stopping for a few pints in the Cat and Cage. It was an amazing experience. You must remember that we are a tiny county, and our only success came with national league and Leinster titles in 1966 and 1968 respectively. Long before I was born. No big games, or big days out, or success celebrations. Now here we were in Drumcondra, shouting across the road: 'Jaysus, howiya, Paddy? Ha? Come on de town!' People who hadn't met for years were reunited; it felt like we were taking over Dublin. Louis J. Belton, knocking back a pint in the doorway of the pub.

'Howiya doin'?'

'Great, Louis. Are you going to play yourself?'

'Bejaysus, I might.'

The roof was lifting off the pub with the Longford Town chants, red and black flags hung out everywhere, Philip Reynolds outside trying to buy headbands for the kids. Even seeing the street vendors selling rip-off Longford merchandise was a novelty not to be forgotten. The mood was already celebratory. The consensus was that we would never be here again, so by Jaysus we were going to enjoy it. Annette was disappointed when we had to leave to go down to Tolka Park. I couldn't stand still with excitement. Wandering down to the ground, bumping into old school friends, almost crying as we thought, 'Jaysus, I love Longford!'

Bohs had already won the league that season and were in amazing form. 'Plucky' Longford were just amazing in that they had survived in the top flight. We played OK, too, there was plenty of heart, but we couldn't score. Bohs had an extra gear and eventually made it tell. The result was 1-0 to Bohs, but we did ourselves proud and celebrated anyway, because as finalists Longford were going to Europe next season! It was an incomparable feeling, not dissimilar to a good election.

And speaking of elections, the 2002 campaign was fast approaching. Peter didn't need my help all that much. My talent was speechmaking, and he had a different kind of meet-the-people campaign planned. And he was keeping things local; my expertise was always national. He did canvass the Fermoyle area with my father, and when it was over he rang me and said that it had been 'the best canvass of the entire election'. Peter was one guy who appreciated the value of local knowledge, and no one had more of that than my father. He knew what way everyone voted – like I said, you can count them from the register. He knew absolutely everybody in the locality, too, and by keeping his ear to the ground could very nearly predict the issues each household would have. My father is one of the finest canvassers there ever was, and he keeps it run to a strict timetable, so you get an enormous area covered. Peter Kelly was around this game long enough to know that that kind of ability is pure gold dust to the candidate. So, if you are running for election, that's the kind of person you need to have on your team in each area.

Don't be fooled by people who say it can't be done in cities: it can, I've seen it. You just need more people, one for every road or estate. It's your job to get out there and recruit them. Forget laptops and graphs, it's about people. It's also true that there is another talent in city elections. You get maybe four or five seconds walking up the driveway to a house; use that time. How old is the car? What size is it? Are there bumper stickers? Are there children's toys in the garden? How is the garden kept? What is the pavement outside the house like? What condition is the house in from the outside? Can you see a television on? What programme is showing? Is there footwear left in the porch? What kind is it, e.g. boots? Is there other election literature in the house?

Take stock of how the door opens. If the hinges are on your right, stand with your right shoulder to the door, and vice versa, Take full stock of the person who opens the door: male, female, young, old, their clothing, Take note of the inside hallway, the furnishings. If you do all that in those few seconds you can almost predict every issue that will be thrown at you, you can understand what makes this person tick. Tailor what you say to suit what you have just learned about them. Focus on what you know they want. People like you to know about their issues. Jump in with a short sharp spiel, catch their attention; if they are ushering you out, ask them if they have any issues they want to raise. Remind them that now is the time – that's what you're here for. Invite them to let you have it! You should be able for it, if you're any kind of candidate. And should all that fail, say something like, 'I see from the toys you have kids. Do you mind me asking what do you think of the schools in the area? I just had a kid myself …' Hook, line and sinker. Even in the worst of elections, I have never had a door slammed in my face. They might not have agreed with me, but I engaged them, gave them food for thought, and if it was possible to get their vote, I'm sure I gave it as good a shot as was humanly possible. I wonder if I would make any money out of setting up a school for canvassers?

Sadly, canvassing is a dying art. Too many people are rushing along, they don't do any of this stuff, they just knock on your door and say 'Give Joe Bloggs your No. 1. Have you any questions? We promise a, b and c.' The door is shut and the literature in the bin before they reach the next house. In 2002 a Labour candidate – a candidate, not just a canvasser – called to my door and asked for my No. 1 vote, and proceeded to tell me all that the government had done wrong. I said nothing. They went away happy. If they had looked at my car they would have seen the Fianna Fáil stickers, and the literature on the back seat, and could at least have hoped for a preference and aimed for that. Needless to say, they weren't elected.

Fianna Fáil canvassers are often just as bad these days. Terrified and nervous when the door opens. Chatting and laughing between houses instead of taking note of what they should. Half-hearted, half-arsed. I know you are probably thinking that my method takes time; rubbish, you make it up with the quick walk between houses. I have never been passed out on a canvass. I am not trying to say I'm perfect here, although sometimes I am forced to defer to popular opinion, but it's just an art I think more people, across all parties, should take the time to learn. It's not all that difficult and it can make a difference.

Although it can be difficult at times, canvassing can also be fun. It's a great way to meet people, both your fellow canvassers and the people on the doorsteps. During the 2002 election, we were canvassing one estate in Lucan with a fairly large team, and as one of the girls approached a house, she saw a woman getting into the passenger side of her car, while her husband rushed back inside to get something they had obviously forgotten. When our intrepid canvasser approached the lady in question, she looked out of the car with a pained expression and said, 'Jesus, not now, I'm having a baby!' It was the first time we accepted the excuse of being in labour as a reason not to listen to our campaign spiel. We left it at that, and hoped she would remember us on election day. I'm sure she did.

When you are canvassing in more rural areas, you would be amazed at how much tea you end up drinking. You find yourself talking about the same things over and over, but people are so nice you politely act surprised and discuss the matter as if you have never heard it mentioned before. Of course, every house thinks that no one will have invited you in. 'Sure, you must be parched. Sit down and have a sup of tea.' You usually make excuses, but some people have the invitation down to a fine art. They get you in the door, where the husband keeps you talking, and before you know it along comes the wife with a tray of tea and biscuits. God bless them, you may not feel like it at the time, but when people are doing something so kind-hearted, what can you say but gulp it down and keep going.

You can't shy away from any door, whether you have to fight through bushes or unlock Krypton Factor gates to get to it. I remember when we were canvassing with Andrea Reynolds in Newtowncashel once, we found one farmer out in his field trying to get sheep into a pen in preparation for a visit by the shearer. We looked over the nine-bar gate and there he was knee deep in mud, dragging one poor sheep by the head. 'Howiya. Sorry I can't come out, I'm busy.' Andrea looked back and said, 'Ah, sure that's no problem. We'll come to you.' He stared in disbelief as the daughter of a Taoiseach hopped the gate, and crossed through the mud in her runners and jeans to give him the flyer and shake his hand. She never batted an eyelid, and you could see the admiration all over his face, as he had wrongly presumed that such a classy girl would never have considered destroying her clothes just to shake his hand and pat the bemused sheep.

Dogs, of course, are an ever-present problem. It's no wonder they terrify postmen. I could have had several claims against ones that snapped at my finger-tips as I put a flyer in a letterbox. I went to a house once and when the door opened there was this Irish wolfhound, standing quite calmly, but even on all fours he was able to look me directly in the eye. I gulped. He looked me up and down before deciding that something that much smaller than him could not pose any risk, and he headed back down the hall. His owner laughed at my expression. 'My God, what do you feed him?' I asked. 'Steak,' he replied. Must cost a bloody fortune, I thought, before discussing at length the virtues of Fianna Fáil and C&D Petfoods in Longford.

It is vitally important never to upset plants in a garden or trample across a lawn; you never know how much work someone has put into it. Gates must be closed after you and everything left as it was. I approached one door in Ranelagh and when I rang the doorbell it made a dreary, dying squawk, and the entire bell came away in my hand. I was in a cold sweat as the door opened, the owner finding me standing there with his broken doorbell in my hand. I thought he was going to be one of those 'I'll get the guards for you' types, but instead he laughed and said 'Ah, it's OK. You're with the right party. Don't worry, it does that all the time.' I walked away meekly, while he fumbled with the problem of putting his doorbell back together.

Doing leaflet drops and flyers is a somewhat easier task, but it's all about speed. It must be done quickly. Even so, care should be taken that leaflets are not left hanging out of a letterbox, as this lets burglars know there is nobody in. If there is a pile of mail inside the door, don't bother adding your flyer to it, it will only annoy the householder. Don't ever stuff it in and jam up their letterbox, and don't leave it where opposition parties can grab it and pull it out if they are doing the area after you – they will do that, too.

Letterboxes are odd things. Some are wide open and friendly, a dream for postmen and leaflet droppers; others are just plain impossible. You get the feeling that the people inside don't want any contact with others. They don't just have brushes, they have hard brushes that you can't get your fingers past, never mind the leaflet, and the inside of the box tears the skin all around your fingers. Don't get me started on those bloody sideways letterboxes that are spring-loaded like a mousetrap. I've nearly lost an arm in those bloody things. How postmen do it, I don't know. Worst of all, though, is when you come to an estate where all the letterboxes are at the bottom of the door. What bright spark thought that up? You spend a week going round like a cripple with a bad back after encountering one of those estates.

No matter what, I would remind everybody out there that canvassers are simply volunteers. They believe in a party and a candidate. In a world where it is increasingly difficult to get a message across, they offer to give up their time to go to your door and talk to you about an election and any issues you may have. They are not robots; they are not decision-makers. They are usually cold, overworked, tired and worn-out listening to arguments. Give them a break. We prize democracy in Ireland; we prize free speech. Yet if tomorrow morning all political parties collapsed, then bang goes your democracy. All political parties in Ireland would cease to function were it not for the work of their volunteers. Next time you see a wet and dishevelled youngster of whatever party approaching your door, upsetting you in the middle of Coronation Street, just think that that innocuous little figure is all that stands between you and autocracy or anarchy.

It's not easy to keep going. In the modern age, there is a lot of bad feeling towards politics and politicians, and you have to use all your charm on the doorstep to get a vote, or even a reaction. But there are some things that help. The odd person who says, 'Yeah, sure, I always vote for them.' The person who has a genuine query and gives you the opportunity to discuss it. The banter and the craic. Most of all it's probably the thought of getting home to a warm house and putting your feet up!

So why do we do it at all? When I was running for the Committee of Fifteen, between work and politics I could be working anywhere up to eighteen or nineteen hours a day. At the best of times you put in several hours of work per week between meetings and other activities. Many members take part of their annual leave from work just so they can help canvass; they arrange holidays around likely election dates. What makes these volunteers want to give up so much of their lives? What do they get out of it? Well as Paul Daniels used to say, 'Not a lot.'

Perhaps I can best explain it this way. Why would someone support Liverpool or Manchester United? Why would they spend hours looking at them on television, join supporters clubs, spend money on merchandise, when at best they will see the team play maybe twice a year, if ever. What do those supporters get out of it? And there you have it. Volunteers to political parties enjoy it. They support their team through thick and thin. They give their time so as when the team wins they can say that they played their part, and they feel part of something greater. The only difference is that most political volunteers also have a strong sense of idealism, and believe that in some small way they are doing their bit to make the world a better place. They might get an odd pint out of their local TD, they probably get a few thank-you letters, but when things go right they get to celebrate and cheer in the same way as people would cheer if Robbie Keane scored the winner in the World Cup final.

For me, well, at the end of the day I sit back and think that, whether you agree with me or not, I did what I thought was right, I did my bit for Ireland. Pearse, Parnell and Wolfe Tone would be proud of me.

11

THE GODDESS VICTORIA

There is always a multitude of reasons why a candidate fails, but it's never easy to take. Des Kelly, a candidate in Lucan who had served on the national executive with me, was a good guy, open and honest, and he put his heart into everything. Des would have made an excellent public representative but, unfortunately, the sheer lack of political organisation in Lucan was against him, and the free rein given to anti-establishment politics was very hard to combat.

We felt that some unfair local media coverage made it tough for Des, and there was also the fact that the local organisation in Lucan was not in good shape. The remnants of the old Liam Lawlor team might be there but, to be honest, a lot had given up after the revelations and the push that forced him from the Dáil. Those still there were willing to work but they lacked any real leadership. No one wanted to take on the task of instituting new cumainn and reorganising the Party right across the Lucan area. Fine Gael was in no better shape. In all, the establishment parties failed to provide any real presence among their members in the community. 'New' parties, like the Greens, benefited from this state of affairs. They were small units, dedicated and eager, unlike their opponents, who had all the appearance of tired, worn-out monoliths. The big parties no longer had the stomach for the fight, while the independents and Greens saw an opportunity to prove themselves. There was a market among the electorate for blame politics, too, and the small parties fed off this. After they were elected, they managed to claim credit for every positive step implemented by the government, while abdicating all responsibility for Lucan's ever increasing problems. You've gotta admire them for it really.

I enjoyed the canvassing, though. It was a great way to get to know a place, especially when you're new to the area, like I was. I think it's important to remember one major factor that I saw on the doorsteps: the popularity of Liam Lawlor. He was no longer standing for election, on account of all the tribunal revelations, but a huge number of people on the doorsteps told me what a shame it was to see him go, and how, whatever else he did, he was a terrible loss to Lucan. Council estates like Arthur Griffith wanted Lawlor back. Well-to-do estates like Roselawn were also adamant that Lawlor was a huge loss. If he had run, I have no doubt that he would have polled a huge vote.

Fianna Fáil played down the fact that he might have been elected, in order to improve their chances, but the truth on the ground was very different. Lawlor may have done dodgy deals, he may have broken rules, he may have conned a few millionaires out of their hard-earned cash, but the people of Lucan felt that Lawlor had done a good job for them. I was amazed. Going out on the canvass, I expected to meet a backlash against Liam Lawlor, when in fact I often ended up trying to explain why the Party had taken such a tough line with him. If his family can take comfort from one thing, I think it should be the knowledge that a large number of people in Lucan remember Liam Lawlor fondly, and remember him as a man who did good work for his constituency. Perhaps people only appreciate someone after they are gone.

I canvassed for a number of candidates and friends around Dublin, and canvassed in Louth for Dermot Ahern. I was probably involved in doing bits and pieces in so many places that I probably wasn't of great assistance to anyone in particular, but for me it was brilliant craic. I certainly never got bored, meeting new teams and people all the time. It was a great experience. And because no one was depending on me there were fewer demands on my time, and I had the freedom to enjoy the election to the full.

It was probably just as well, because this was also the first general election since I began dating Annette. When you are involved in a political party and an election hits, it takes up every night of every week for at least three weeks. You canvass, you listen to radio and television, you attend meetings; you do leaflet drops and check postering, come hail, rain or even sunshine. You give it every ounce of energy you've got. Family lives suffer, as everything in the household centres around the election, and so do personal relationships. Volunteers make a huge sacrifice for the democratic process, one that is completely unappreciated by the general public.

2002 was also an incredibly easy election. There is no other way of putting it. 1992 was a slog, as were the ones in the late 1980s. 1997 was a bit of an anti-climax, but 2002 was essentially just a breeze. The economy was an astounding success, and the coalition had a good record in almost every area of government. OK, there were problems in some sectors, like the health service, but even here the truth was that funding had been increased beyond all recognition, and people had to give credit for that. A lot done, more to do. Whoever thought up that slogan should get a lifetime achievement award. It got canvassers out of many a scrape on a doorstep, and created a vision everyone could relate to. Every office meeting, every school board meeting, every sports commentator can still find use for that slogan. It has entered folklore.

Confidence was high in Fianna Fáil. To this day people talk about the Party's slick media campaign, and it was good, but that was not the reason Fianna Fáil was so successful. A number of people talked up the media campaign in order to explain the result, and Fianna Fáil, wanting to be seen as professional, allowed the story to grow. But the real seeds of our success were to be seen at the Árd Fheis: sheer confidence. The members were chomping at the bit, itching to get out on the doorsteps. We were fighting fit, ready for anything. No tiredness, fatigue, or disillusionment; just pride and self-belief. Everyone was well informed, interested and up to speed. Deirdre Heney, who was a candidate that year, remarked on it when we spoke, and we whispered the words 'overall majority' softly in each other's ears, as if talking of the love that dare not speak its name.

The Party's self-confidence could be summed up by an interview my father gave to The Week in Politics, when a reporter asked him what did he think of the Labour Party's comments that they could not see themselves going into government with Fianna Fáil. Oh, yes, he liked a question like that. He rubbed his hands and said, 'The Labour Party ought to have some manners and wait until someone asks them to go into government. Whoever said that Fianna Fáil wants them?'

And that was the attitude of most members. They knew that it was highly unlikely that Fianna Fáil would need to approach Labour in any form after an election, and their pompous posturing about whether or not they would enter a government with Fianna Fáil only made delegates blood boil. They still hadn't forgotten 1994, you know.

It reminded me of a conversation I had with Ruairí Quinn while I was on the Fianna Fáil national executive. We were all drinking in the Dáil bar and a lot of Labour people were there from some Party function. Towards the end of the night Damian Murphy and myself happened to get talking to Ruairí Quinn. He was all chat and, to be honest, he was one of the Labour people that I liked, even after his 'we want a head' episode in 1994. I told him of how well I thought the government had been working that year and that it was a shame it fell. He agreed that it was a good government but added, 'So was the one after,' with a wry smile. I promptly reminded him that Labour would give their life's blood to have Fianna Fáil's record of having every piece of major legislation protecting workers' rights brought in under their governments.

'Not all of it,' Quinn responded, 'but I'll give you the point that a lot has been.'

'So, doesn't it make sense that one day we will end up in government again?' I said. At this point, the palsy-walsy nature of our chat took a turn, and Quinn proceeded to tell me that that could only happen when Fianna Fáil cleaned up their act, improved the moral standard – all this stuff, ad nauseum. Now that's fine for the television, but not where a politician should know better. I looked at him and said:

'Remember this, Fianna Fáil is not about a few fellas. It's tens of thousands of decent, honest, hardworking people, and by taking that sanctimonious attitude you insult me and all of them. Yes, there is no room for corruption, but there is no room either for insulting and blackening the names of good people the length and breadth of the country. And I can tell you one thing, Ruairí, I won't be lectured on morals or standards by anyone in the Labour Party.'

To his credit, he said that of course the majority of people in Fianna Fáil were good and decent and he did not mean to attack them – it was the actions of certain individuals he was aiming at. But the truth was that he did attack them with his blanket assertions about the nature of the Party.

We left on good terms, but the encounter convinced me that we still were not ready to go into power with Labour. They had yet to learn about dealing with people, and put aside their pompous, holier-than-thou attitude.

The fact that I have spent this long talking about Labour and not yet mentioned Fine Gael speaks volumes. No one was talking about them. Michael Noonan had taken over but had bombed. Labour was acting as the opposition.

We stayed down in Longford for election day. My days of canvassing at the school may have been gone, but I still loved the banter with Pat Brennan, who would be there for the Blueshirts, and the craic of the polling station. The day of the count was amazing. It was revenge for 1992; it was 1987 all over again. Electronic voting was used in Dublin West, Meath and Dublin North, and these early counts provided a taste of the success that would follow. Nora Owens' loss, meanwhile, spelled impending disaster for the Blueshirts.

I'm a big fan of electronic voting, even if it kills the fun of the counts. It's more accurate; simple as that. Our paper system can't count every vote in a surplus or elimination, they just take a sample.

It's usually an accurate guess but, let's face it, if you lose a seat by three votes you want to know every possible vote has been counted. My major gripe with those who objected to electronic voting when Martin Cullen tried to introduce it later on, was that they never apply the same rules and tests to the system we currently have. If you did, you would come to the conclusion that, despite its faults, electronic voting is safer. The fact that some people still consider our paper system safer and more reliable than electronic voting is just incredible.

I once had someone tell me that, because Party members can observe the count and make their point while votes are being counted, this means our system is fair and above board. Anyone who thinks that has never been at a count. Make a point? I had one counter tell me to 'fuck off' when I told her a vote had been placed in an incorrect bundle. Add to this the fact that it's bloody difficult to keep pace with the votes, and you are simply trying to get tallies. It's only when things go to the wire that you get any real say in the counting process. The manual vote is inaccurate, open to abuse, open to corruption and costly – the same allegations that people make against electronic voting.

But, of course, once the 'smart arses' got on to the idea, they destroyed electronic voting. Their wild talk of corruption and people stealing and swapping the disks and so on and so forth is just ridiculous. There is not enough money in Irish politics to make such a risk worthwhile, and I have yet to meet a politician of any party who I would deem capable of doing it. They all take great pride in their mandate, and though many dirty tricks or strokes may be used, no politician is going to falsify the entire vote. I could not imagine even the most corrupt or misguided among us ever seriously contemplating it. It would be too easy to catch them out, anyway, and that would bring ruin on any such politician and his party.

But, getting back to the count and election 2002, there was such a buzz about our house – there was a buzz everywhere. The results were beginning to flow in and all over the country it was Fianna Fáil leading the way. Oh, how sweet. My father sat in his armchair, grinning like a Cheshire cat, and greeting each result with 'Oh, Jaysus, that's a sight,' due the level of Fianna Fáil success, on the one hand, and the annihilation of the Blueshirts, on the other. We were winning seats everywhere, seats that we had no right to win. My good friend, reporter Nick Coffey, was on the television insisting that it would be an overall majority, while my other good friend, P. J. Mara, sat shaking his head, saying, 'I've spent too many late nights crying bitter tears to believe that.' He was right: dreaming the impossible dream at this point was just going to torture yourself.

Still, Fianna Fáil was like the cat that got the cream. Everything was right. Michael Noonan had resigned as Fine Gael leader by the afternoon. The PDs were having a good election, and in the end it was they who denied us the overall majority, just like in 1987. When we took eighty-one seats – oh, so close – we cracked open the champagne in our house and made a night of it. We just couldn't believe how good it was. We narrowly failed to take three seats in Longford–Roscommon, losing out to the PDs again, but Fianna Fáil's success right around the country was such a phenomenal performance in this day and age that I don't think anyone cared. Bertie raising his hands in delight, my father with tears in his eyes as the final results came in, my mother whooping with glee and doing a little dance on the floor every so often. Annette was bemused by the whole thing, and tired from lack of sleep as the results and celebrations carried on into the late hours.

We were back. Nothing could stop us now. Peter Kelly was elected, Donie Cassidy was elected, Mary O'Rourke lost out, but Conor Lenihan managed to help pull an extra seat for Charlie O'Connor. Pat Rabbitte, who had by now joined the Labour Party, was left fighting Fine Gael's Brian Hayes for a last seat in Dublin South West. Rabbitte was elected but without reaching the quota: kick in the teeth there.

This was what it's all about: victory. Strutting around for a couple of weeks afterwards, accepting the accolades. In no time at all it's history, of course, and new problems arise to give everyone ammunition to throw at you. That's life. Politics must end in failure, because even in the ultimate vindication of an election victory, there will be new challenges to confront, new issues to be sorted. Within a month of the result, the media and opposition were already talking about the pasting Fianna Fáil would get at the next election. That may come some day, but it's almost twenty five years since the country voting as a whole has returned an alternative to Fianna Fáil to power. That's some endorsement.

To be honest, I felt sorry for some of the Blueshirts. I know people who have been in Fine Gael who don't know what it's like to win a general election and go into government on the back of it. They didn't deserve to lose some of their seats, it must be said. The opposition was a mess, too divided among too many parties. The Greens did well, taking five seats, but they took them off Fine Gael, thereby weakening the opposition even further. Sinn Féin made big gains, according to the papers. Guys, get a grip. Five seats? We narrowly lost out on twice that amount. It was like watching a soccer match where a bunch of amateurs loses to AC Milan, 81–5, and the reporters at the game try to say it's a victory for the amateurs because they scored five goals.

Sinn Féin's Martin Ferris took Dick Spring's seat. Now, in our house we couldn't help but enjoy a wry smile at seeing Dick Spring get his comeuppance after what he did to Albert, but we knew that the result was not for the best. Radical politics never solves problems, and Sinn Féin was all radicalism. Much as we hated the Blueshirts, they had some semblance of responsibility, because they knew they might have to deliver in government one day. Sinn Féin and the Greens, on the other hand, made up policies without any regard for the country as far as we could see. They could afford to do so because they would never have to be in government, and even if they were they would be the smaller party and could abdicate responsibility at that point too. That was our belief, still is and probably always will be. The same way they think we are evil, hold regular meetings with the devil himself, and take backhanders everywhere we can.

Annette was teaching in Bray at this stage and I had great sport rubbing it into some of the teachers at her school's summer party. Annette had a very difficult commute to work, however, and it was very damaging to her health. It was thirty miles to Bray and thirty miles back. As is often the case, it isn't the drive itself that causes the problems, even though it was across the Wicklow mountains, it's the associated stress. Pushing to be there on time, not knowing what conditions would be like crossing the hills on an icy morning; the pressure to brave anything to get to work, and the feeling most employees have that if they are late or cannot make it, no one will believe them. It was really taking a heavy toll on her and she was in hospital more than once with various problems. Her doctor, Tony Feeney, one of the best GPs you could find, continually raged at the disgraceful way the M50 was held up by a group of tree hugging hippies – because of the butt of an old wall which had been dug up that had little or no historical significance.

We now have professional protestors who manage to block the streets of Dublin, before shooting out to the Glen of the Downs, then on to Shannon and back up to Rossport just to stick a placard in the air. Where do they get the time? Sure, they haven't a job between the lot of them, so in other words our taxes fund this protesting – and then they often have the cheek to call themselves Socialist Workers! But, as Dr Feeney pointed out, surely the cars parked along the M50 emitting CO_2 were doing more damage to the environment than Carrickmines was saving. It also took no account of people like Annette who were suffering because of it. To say we were all fuming about this stupid controversy would be an understatement.

As soon as the summer had passed, the media went on the attack. During the election, they criticised us for being too vague and for not making any substantial promises, for being miserly with what we did promise, and for having too many caveats about the performance of the economy. Now the papers were filled with stories of how we had broken promises (it was a five-year plan and we weren't five months in power), for promising too much and being too carefree with spending, and for not taking the economic situation into account. You can't win. Then came the stories about cuts. The thing I never will understand about government is, when you increase spending by 10 per cent one year, and the following increase it by eight per cent, this further increase can be described as a two per cent cut? It makes no sense whatsoever. It is typical old-fashioned public sector thinking, which holds that you have to keep increasing the increases or else it's a cut. Ridiculous!

Volunteers use the period between elections to prepare for the next campaign, whenever that might occur. You keep informed and up to speed. You attend meetings. You try to make sure that people get to know your party's views, so they will understand matters when the time comes. You focus on the positives and keep reminding people of them. You attend more meetings. You attend a few fundraisers, the occasional dinner-dance, followed by a meeting or two. I remember a man from Clare telling me at great length all about a book he had just read. 'Where do you get all the time for reading?' I asked him. He looked back at me quite seriously and said, 'Sure, that's what you do when there isn't an election on.'

That December we attended the Taoiseach's dinner, one of the social highlights of the political year, when all the great and the good of Fianna Fáil come out for a huge Christmas bash. It's one occasion when the politicians can afford to let their hair down. The dinner clashed with Annette's birthday, but it was such a good night that she never minded. I found her chatting with Charlie McCreevy, a man described by a good friend of ours as being 'stranger than truth'. He was a legend, a brilliant politician. He opposed Haughey, and accepted his subsequent banishment to the back-benches as punishment. He never left the Party. He stood by it, and when

Albert brought him back, did he criticise Haughey? No, not even amid the mud slinging of recent years. He was in fact one of the few brave enough to remind people of some of the good things Haughey had done. McCreevy had a brilliant financial mind and made a superb minister for finance. I never tired of watching RTÉ economics correspondent George Lee reach boiling point at every budget, fumbling over figures, so obviously annoyed that McCreevy had outwitted him again, and come up with an unexpected proposal. Not that Charlie would gloat about that. Oh, no, he still loved to play the lock-keepers son who had no shoes on his feet. 'I am what I am, *garsún*,' he would say. You couldn't help but admire his class.

12

SUCCESS OF A DIFFERENT KIND

Over the course of the next year, Annette developed serious back problems, and was over and back to the doctor on a continual basis. Physiotherapy didn't work, exercise didn't work, rest certainly didn't work. She ended up on heavy painkillers, a situation that was far from satisfactory. She was also getting very depressed by the whole thing.

I have to admit that I wasn't a whole lot of help. As regards the back problem, I would do what I would, but it was when she was depressed that she needed my help most. I guess I learned then that I would never make a counsellor. My problem is that I have no concept of, or empathy for the basic problems of depression. I used to think I did, but when you are close to someone you really begin to understand how useless you are. I have never been depressed, sure I get down, but never depressed. My emotions have always been a light switch; all I ever needed was someone to help take my mind off things, to go for a drink or just do something, and I could snap out of it. I would try to cheer Annette up, but then I got annoyed when nothing I did worked, even though there was nothing she could do to help it. Her depression and her seeming inability to forget her problems and have fun would annoy me. I just don't know what to do in that situation because I have no way of understanding what is going on, and my happy-go-lucky nature is probably the last thing someone wants around.

Compounding the problems was the fact that Dad suffered another heart attack. When we went to see him it was clear that he was very weak and not the man we had known. He was sent to the Mater hospital in Dublin to have a stent put in his artery, an operation no one would wish to undergo. The stent is something which helps to widen the artery and hold it open. The doctors and staff in both the Mater and Mullingar were fantastic, and after about two weeks in hospital he was sitting up in bed, complaining about the state of the world and giving politics a good lashing. Once we heard him arguing, Annette and I looked at each other and said, 'Yes, he's back.'

In October, I decided to take a big step and go back to college. I had avoided it for years, thinking up all manner of excuses to avoid giving up my evenings in the name of further study. I mean, I was never the most studious guy, never mind trying to work and study at the same time. All jobs seem to want you to take up night courses, and I had been plagued for years with people encouraging me to do banking, taxation or accounting exams. I managed to avoid them all, but now I decided that I needed a more particular qualification, something to fall back on. Something that would tie in with work in the government affairs area. I thought a diploma in public relations might just suit.

The Irish Academy of PR ran the most accessible lectures two nights a week out in UCD, and I signed up, hoping I wasn't too long out of the system to be beyond studying. I was nervous the first night I went out to UCD. The place was so enormous for a start, I reckoned I was lucky that I hadn't gone to college there, because I don't think I would have lasted. You can't help having a kind of inferiority complex when you visit these places. I must admit that I didn't sense the same snootiness as I had at Trinity, though there was definitely an air of the intelligentsia about the place all the same. Then again, this time I was there to study and always went straight from work dressed in a suit. Maybe that made a difference.

Public relations held a certain attraction for me because of its importance in politics. It gets a bad name – a lot of people dismiss it as 'spin' – but it does play a very important role. A PR person is responsible for breaking down a message and making sure that it reaches the public in a form they can understand. If you just throw a message or policy out there, detractors will throw up smokescreens and red herrings and obscure the issue until it is lost. Therefore you employ PR to make sure your message is watertight, that it will get to the public, and that it can be understood. Of course, when your PR is so good that this is exactly what happens, your detractors will tell everyone it's 'spin'. You know you have done something right when all your opponents can say is, 'This is a PR stunt. It's all just spin.' That's to say, 'Feck, I can't find any holes in it. It's exactly what should be done, but I'm not going to admit that, am I?'

I settled into the course in no time. I immediately became one of those creatures of habit who must sit in the same seat every week, and soon made friends with Jennifer Jones and Breda Keane, while Catherine Maguire from IBEC was also in this circle. Dave Coleman, who worked as press officer for the revenue, also became a good friend during the course. Having good friends on a course makes it much easier to give up those Tuesday and Thursday nights, though night-classes are still tough going. There is no worse feeling than running straight out of work to head into two-and-a-half hours of college on a wet winter's evening. Sometimes, just staying awake is an achievement. Then you realise you have to do this for two years.

We did have one brilliant respite, though. Against all the odds and against all our beliefs, Longford Town ended up in the FAI cup final once again. This time the match was to be played in Lansdowne Road. We couldn't believe it. Their league form was never scintillating – when you went to a game you never knew whether they would wipe out the opposition or fall to a crushing defeat – but our cup form was something else. When we beat Galway in the semi-final it was like a dream come true.

I got two tickets for the final, but Annette's back was so bad it didn't look like she could go. On the day of the match, however, she appeared at the top of the stairs as I was heading out the door. 'I don't want to be alone,' she said. 'Maybe I could go and see how I get on.' She had grown to like the excitement and thrill of live football. So I hugged her and said, 'Sure. Look, come in to the game, and if you feel like you are in too much pain at any stage, just head home.'

Annette agreed to go on the basis that I would stay on if she left, as she didn't want to ruin my day, because lately she felt as if she was ruining things for everyone she knew.

We met up with Pádraig Loughrey, my old debating team-mate and probably the shrewdest young political mind in Longford, who by now had set up his own pharmacy in the town. The atmosphere in the Waterloo pub was brilliant. It was so crowded you had to queue for a urinal in the men's jacks, and one St. Patrick's fan vacating a spot said to me. 'There you go, that's the last thing we will let you have today.'

It was amazing to see Dublin swamped by Longfordians once more, and the supporters on both sides made sure their presence was felt in Lansdowne. Sure, we were here for the craic again, although this time a little more confident. From the kick-off it was clear Longford were up for it. Every ball contested, every tackle won; St Pat's just didn't show up at all. Then it happened – the ball came down to Seánie Francis, who dropped his shoulder, ran and chipped the ball, high and dropping down for an eternity, a St Pat's defender rushing towards it but too late … goal! The stand went crazy, everyone hugging each other – we were pushed forward several rows, children laughing, young fellas screaming, grown men crying with delight, women kissing everyone around them, shouting till the vocal chords ripped! That excited feeling in the pit of your stomach, that sense of sheer euphoria.

In the midst of this madness, I thought of poor Annette – she had swallowed a few painkillers with a whisky in the pub – and I turned to try to find her. She was hugging some old man who had tears rolling down his cheeks, a bit too much to drink, and thinking all his birthdays had come at once. When the crowd finally settled down, Annette looked at me and said, 'I know my back will probably pay for this later, but right now it's fine, and that was the best cure ever. Better than any drug. I never enjoyed anything so much.' Neither did I, but I was doubly satisfied by the fact that she was beginning to see why men like football, and that was something she could only ever understand through live football, and through seeing what it meant to the people of Longford.

The rest of the match was great, Barry Ferguson, the Longford captain missed a penalty that would have put us all at ease, but other than that Longford kept the pressure up and Pat's chances were few and far between. I never enjoyed a match so much, because Pat's never really got going and never threatened, so for Longford fans it was very enjoyable. When Pat's threw caution to the wind in the final moments, Eric Lavine got a breaking ball and raced upfield – even Annette was screaming 'shoot, shoot' – but he held back, squared the ball, and the following strike rebounded off the post. Minutes later, another break. This time Shane Barrett made no mistake, and the crowd went wild a second time. With only seconds remaining on the clock, the chant 'champione, champione are we' rang out from the stand. Meself and Loughrey hugged each other and then as the cup was lifted I held Annette in my arms and thought that life just couldn't possibly get any better.

I rang Dad, who was watching the game on television, and I could hear the tears of joy in his voice, my mother cheering in the background. We stayed in the stadium for ages, then walked out onto the streets, still singing, smiles as broad as O'Connell Street on the faces of every Longford fan. The bemused drivers of Dublin city held up by the crowd, regardless of the colour of the traffic light. Every so often the night air of leafy Dublin 4 was pierced by a cry of 'Come on de tooooowwwn' which would be answered by a cacophony of car horns and flag-waving. It reminded me of the cartoon a paper carried when Albert was elected Taoiseach. A well-to-do couple were walking in Dublin 4, and the woman turned to the man and said, 'Darling, where is this place, Longford?' Well, they knew tonight, I can tell you; the answer was right there on their doorstep.

As Annette and I ducked into Burger King for a bite to eat, a couple of St Pat's kids shouted 'boggers' at us (if only they knew, Annette was possibly more dub than them!). I politely reminded them that we were boggers with a cup, and to their credit they just laughed and enjoyed the banter. There were several Longford fans on the bus back to Lucan, all either staying or living in Lucan, and a few Pat's fans as well, and the banter started up between them. It was all good fun, the way football should be. One of the kids from Pat's started to draw on the condensation of the bus window, the usual thing of a sheep being chased by a Longford man, but in trying to illustrate the point he gave his character the most enormous willy.

'Now, that's what I like to see,' a Longford fan remarked, 'a good drawing done to scale.'

We had arranged to meet our friends, Tara and Paddy, for a few that night in Leixlip. Tara had been Annette's friend since they were kids, and Paddy and I got on great as he was a kindred soul, being a culchie from Donegal dating a Lucan girl. We went to the Three Sisters pub and got plastered. I insisted on wearing my Town jersey and people just kept coming up to congratulate me. We were in Kildare now, and they loved to stick it to the Dubs too. Even the band played a few songs especially for me. So this is what it's like to win. No wonder the Kerry and Meath crowd love it so much.

After the excitement died down, though, Annette found herself suffering even more with her back and went to see a consultant. He sent her for scans but said the results were not conclusive – he wouldn't feel safe operating and therefore exercise was the only option. Annette took to the exercise regime with real commitment, determined to get better.

That December we decided that we were all set to get married. You always imagine a big romantic gesture, something to sweep the girl off her feet, but that wasn't the case for us. To begin with, I had asked Annette to marry me the very first night we met, so I guess she was in no doubt about my intentions. Seriously, though, it was no shock. It was something we had long anticipated. It was clear to us both that we were in love, and it was only natural that we would get married eventually. We had already bought a house together, if you are living together then marriage is only the next step.

It never ceases to amaze me how people in movies or on television go on. Take a couple living together, sharing everything, having great sex, then one day the man turns around and says, 'I love you', at which point the woman looks as if this is the biggest moment in her life. How different reality is. Imagine sleeping with an Irish girl, then you decide to move in, you share everything, from cars to rounds, and are mad about each other. Then you turn around and say, 'I love you' – what do you think the reaction will be? If you are lucky she will just reply 'Luv ya, too,' and not pass any heed. If you insisted on making a big deal about it at this point, you would probably be beaten around the head with the nearest blunt instrument while she screams, 'I should feckin' hope so! Do you mean you never loved me before now? Why, you little shit …'

The lack of romance was probably down to my political nature as well. It's not that I'm afraid to take a risk, but I like to try to ensure I'm in as favourable a position as possible before making my move. My cautious side made sure that there would be no announcement until enough kites had been flown to check that the reaction was favourable.

On Christmas Day 2003 we got engaged. We had a bit of a house party, and all Annette's friends came, along with Keith, Niamh, Sylvia and Natalie from my job. It was a great night, and nothing better than having friends to share it with. In fact, although these guys in my job hadn't got a political bone between the lot of them, they were the best group I had ever worked with. We were all great friends as well as colleagues. We were all on the same team, under the guidance of Karen Martin, who was just as mad as the rest of us. We all worked well together and looked out for each other, no matter what anyone else said or did.

At this point, I should mention another great problem the culchie living in Dublin faces. Christmas. Like many workers, I usually work right up to Christmas Eve, when the office closes. So, you finally finish work, usually exhausted, dying for a break, and find yourself driving in bad conditions and terrible traffic to get back down the country. I had done this for years, but now things were different. I wouldn't be alone in Dublin, I would be with Annette. Having spent Christmas Day in her family's house, we would both drive down to Longford on Stephen's Day and celebrate Christmas all over again with my family.

You might say we had the best of both worlds, but, as I soon found out from more experienced culchies, there is no winning in this situation. Many friends of mine have had the same troubles. I often felt pulled in every direction. My folks were upset if I wasn't able to get home for Christmas day itself, especially my Mam – Dad seemed more worried about the driving. Eventually, I had to swallow a bitter pill, as other culchies advised me, and forget about pleasing people and do what suited me, because, no matter what, someone was going to get hurt. Sure, we could rotate Christmas like some people did, but that just meant risking life and limb to get to Longford on Christmas Eve – and doing the same thing in reverse on Stephen's Day. No, the best solution was to take my rest, then Annette's family got to see us on Christmas Day, and my folks got to see us on Stephens day and for three or four days after to make up for Christmas itself. Then we finally would get a day or two to ourselves. It's hard coming from the country. You never get away from the heartbreak of having had to leave your family 'back home'.

When news came through that Martin Mackin was leaving the post of Fianna Fáil general secretary, I thought about applying for the job. After the success of the 2002 election, there wasn't much else Martin could achieve, and he was interested in moving into public relations consultancy and government affairs.

The role of general secretary is an incredibly tough job. The hours are very long, you have only a small staff, and the vast majority of people in the Party don't have to listen or take orders from you – they are volunteers. Dealing with volunteers is never easy because they will quite rightly only do what they believe in, and will not be driven or accept undue pressure. More than that, as head of the HQ machine, the general secretary is often seen as the leader of the establishment set in Dublin, always trying to put one over on the membership. The general membership believe that the HQ should be looking after them, representing their view and interests, not imposing views from above.

TDs, for their part, see HQ as an extension of their own offices. HQ should support them and know its place – that is, answerable to the elected politician. Councillors and national executive see HQ as their communication link, and woe betide when that link fails to keep them as up to date with developments as they would like to be. Government ministers see HQ as helpful at times, but more often a nuisance, cutting across their role as ministers to haul them back into parish hall politics.

In truth, HQ is all things to all people, and the general secretary is HQ's whipping boy. In an ideal world, the general secretary's role would be to look after the membership, to ensure that the organisation as a whole was well informed and active, to be the voice and conscience of the Party. To let everyone know what the ordinary Joes on the ground will or will not accept. However, in order for that to be the case, the general secretary would have to be allowed to have the influence of a minister, and that just isn't going to happen. Until TDs and ministers find someone who they believe truly puts the Party above all other interests, someone whose moral credentials and love of the Party is beyond question, someone who will only ever act in the best interests of the Party, they will never give in to HQ.

Does such a person exist? Who knows, but if so he or she is probably like Cato in the late Roman Republic, respected, admired and feared by all. And in the end, for all his morals, Cato made a mess of things too, and wasn't above petty prejudice either, so maybe such a person cannot exist after all.

Anyway, I took a bit of time to decide about going for the position. After all, if I were successful, it would be a life-changing experience. I would rarely be home. I would be travelling the country, constantly under the spotlight within the Party, and I needed to know if Annette was ready for that change, especially when she was so ill. She weighed it up and said she knew that this was a role that would make me happy, and that was good enough for her.

I immediately got the CV together and applied for the job. I had applied in 1997 and been called for interview but hadn't done much about it, and being only twenty-one at the time was not really in contention. This time I was taking no chances. I wanted to really give it a run. I knew that I needed to let everyone know that I was in the race and that my CV was strong both in terms of my Party experience and my private sector work, particularly in the area of government affairs. Many, many TDs were extremely supportive and helpful. I met Chris Wall and spent an evening over at his house going through my ideas for the role, all the while taking his advice on board. We have similar thinking on most issues, and his advice was invaluable to me. Chris is an amazing man, a real Party worker who has seen the cut-and-thrust of politics more than most. He has been at Bertie Ahern's right hand for all of his career, and is often portrayed as his fixer or minder, but he is far more than that. Chris is often the man who has the unenviable task of talking sense into people, and that includes the Taoiseach, if needs be. He and his wife, Myra, who works for Dermot Ahern, are two great friends of ours.

Minister Noel Dempsey also helped, and Minister of State Mary Wallace was just tremendous. We met in the Dáil one night and she, being a former human resources manager, took my CV apart and ran through exactly the type of questioning I would face. My old friend Peter Kelly got on to absolutely everybody about me. Conor Lenihan talked to me about what backbenchers would seek from a general secretary. Brian Crowley MEP was his usual optimistic and helpful self, giving any advice he could from a European perspective.

It was clear from feedback and the process itself that this time

I was a contender. Phoenix magazine mentioned my name, which kind of blew any cover I had with my own job, but I have to say everyone was supportive. At one stage, I was informed that the contest was down to three people. I was probably third, but one of the candidates was deemed not to have enough connections with Fianna Fáil, while having a bit too much with another party. That left two of us, or at least that's what informed sources told me afterwards.

The final interview was interesting. I had a good relationship with Pat Farrell, a former general secretary of the Party himself and Louth TD Seamus Kirk who was chairman of the parliamentary party, they were both on the panel, but nonetheless it didn't work out for me. Seamus Kirk rang to let me know the decision. He said that I had come very close (story of my life, don't ya think?) and that one day I would make a fine Árd Rúnaí, but that I was just a bit young and needed a bit more experience right now. Seamus is a great guy, and I appreciated him telling me the story straight. I was very happy that I had come that far, and proved my own standing in the Party, if only to myself, but on the other hand I was devastated that all the ideas and plans I had for the Party would not be happening now. I was sorry because I had really felt and believed that I could restore the faith of the membership and rebuild the bridges and trust between them and HQ. It wouldn't have been easy, but I reckoned I was the one to reinvigorate the people on the ground.

Later I met with Denis O'Connor from Pricewaterhouse-Coopers, who had handled the selection process. He was a very shrewd and smart guy and I appreciated his honesty. He told me straight out that, if I had been the other side of thirty, things might have been different, but that it would have been hard to justify appointing someone as young as me at that particular time.

Shortly after that, it was announced that Seán Dorgan had been appointed general secretary. I have met Seán several times since then and I can see why he got the job. He is a strong guy with the courage of his convictions, and a very able and personable fellow. He's doing a fine job at HQ, even if some of what he does would be different to my approach, though that's not to say I'm right! I have to say I think he has been a great appointment for the Party. We became good friends and have had many great discussions about the future of the Party ever since.

13

ROLL WITH THE PUNCHES

The local and European elections were all the talk for 2004, and it was clear that Fianna Fáil was going to get a very tough time.

The first thing I should say is that, while it saves money and helps ensure a higher turnout, I am absolutely opposed to the idea of having polling for separate elections on the same day. Firstly, European candidates of all parties get feck-all support from the cumainn during a European election, because everyone is so obsessed with what is happening locally. Secondly, the issues about representation at Europe – and there actually are some important ones – get completely lost as the debate squeezes out European matters in favour of local ones. Thirdly, being successful in one election does not mean you will be successful in the other, but if you are in for a tough time you can be sure that losses in one will be reciprocated in the second.

Finally, we should not base elections on when we are likely to get a vote out. If people care enough, they will vote: we shouldn't be going around facilitating people who just can't be bothered. No matter where I have had to come from or what I have had to do, I have always managed to vote on polling day. The only thing we should do is to encourage employers to facilitate all staff who need to vote, and allow them time to do so. Let's face it, employers get an easy time of it when it comes to supporting democracy. They can discourage staff from getting involved in politics, they can shy away from being associated in any way with a political party or supporting an event, because they want to be neutral, and they generally get the hump about allowing people an hour off so as they can vote. I can tell you, employers could do more for the democratic process than anyone if they allowed staff to leave work an hour early in order to vote, so long as they could prove the next day that they went to the polls. You would have an enormous turnout if they did.

I also believe in a 'three strikes and you're out' rule. If a person fails to exercise their democratic right on three consecutive occasions, they should be taken off the register – they have insulted the entire basis of our democracy. Oh yes, I can hear all the smart-arses and bleeding hearts saying that they are entitled not to vote, and that it's the politicians fault for being so boring. Balls! It's your own fault for being too lazy to get off your arse and vote, and for not bothering to involve yourself enough to find out whether a candidate is good, bad or indifferent. Are you so much smarter than all the people who do vote? No, you're not. It's a simple rule. We have the freedom to choose whether or not to vote, but to choose not to vote is to abuse that freedom.

I wasn't involved with the elections at all down home in the Ballymahon local electoral area. I figured I was tainted from the last time and I wanted to let someone else have a go at fixing the mess. In other words, I was older and wiser. Neither of the previous candidates from my area of Cashel, Fermoyle, Lanesboro were running; instead, a former head of Ógra in Longford, Mark Casey, and the cumann chairman in Cashel, Barney Casey, were in the ring. It was generally agreed that only one of them could be nominated, as only four candidates were to contest the election.

This was my first worry. I believed that we should have run four candidates in 1999, when we ran five. The result was a crushing 4–2 victory for Fine Gael. Now, with only two sitting councillors, we had to unseat one of the Blueshirts. Therefore I believed that only three candidates should run this time.

I knew the argument about needing candidates down the table in order to pick up transfers, but our transfers between candidates were ridiculously weak, so I didn't think the transfer argument held water. And the Blueshirts were getting four out of four, so our problem was that, with so many candidates and the Fine Gael vote strong, we were leaving our vote too small. As a result, Fine Gael was taking the seats while we were eliminated. I believed it was possible to level the game at three all, if we ran three candidates. However, I did not make any forceful argument this time; it wasn't my place. I felt it was up to someone else now.

Mick Cahill, who was assistant director of elections in 1999, was running, as were John Nolan and Barney Steele. The Fermoyle cumann where my parents had votes was stuck between Mark Casey and Barney Casey. But we lived in the parish of Cashel and it was natural that Barney Casey should rely on us. I didn't have a vote myself (isn't that handy?) but I have been friends with Barney, his son, Bernard, and, daughter Geraldine, for years, and they were great supporters of mine in my national executive campaign. Politics is about favours and debts, and it was entirely natural that he should call in this one. I gave him my support, and the Fermoyle cumann voted for him, too, but in the end Mark Casey had a greater impact on the other cumainn and won the convention. Ardagh cumann were furious that their candidate lost out to John Nolan, the sitting councillor, who had to be added to the ticket, but that too was a natural choice. Let me explain what happened here.

HQ decided that the convention would pick three candidates; a fourth would then be added to the list. The fourth was either John Nolan or the guy from Ardagh. HQ picked Nolan, which made sense: he was a sitting councillor. This measure of allowing conventions to select only three candidates, while HQ added another (or whatever way the number of candidates worked), was meant to ensure that a sitting councillor would not be cast aside, and then added as an extra candidate for shame's sake. So, you might say, that all makes sense and sounds like good planning.

However, this is what I don't understand. The plan makes sense. Local people on the ground are sensible people. But what they don't like is being dictated to. You can lead the Fianna Fáil faithful, but you can't drive them. It is beyond me why everything HQ does is so often done under a veil of secrecy. No one at the convention was informed of what was happening until they arrived that night to cast their vote. It was not difficult for someone to attend a meeting beforehand, explain the process and the reasons for it, take the flak, and face down the questions. Surely we have people who are capable of doing that? I can tell you that if Brian Cowen arrived at a meeting, explained what was happening and answered the questions, it would have all been accepted. Not that I would suggest a minister should do this, but there must be people capable of it in HQ. If not, we should be employing someone to do it.

You are coasting for a row when you make a decision and fail to inform people of it until the last moment. It creates conspiracy theories in people's minds. We are all trying to win an election, and every little thing should be done in a completely open and transparent way, in consultation with the membership and their representatives on the executive. What's more, when you make a decision like this, the national executive member and the local TD should be in a position to back you up, and be there to help explain it. It speaks volumes that when you visit the websites of Irish political parties, there is not one that gives a list of the staff working in HQ, their responsibilities and their contact details. So much so that there is not a single political party that can say its membership is fully aware of everyone in HQ and understands what they do. This breeds distrust. No matter how good a candidate may seem, how much sense the strategy makes, you cannot impose a decision on a local organisation without consulting them.

Local knowledge is a powerful thing and must be taken into account, but even more importantly, it must be seen to be taken into account. A few phone-calls are not enough; meetings must be held with a full and open debate. Head office personnel in all parties are very often the architects of their own downfall among members on the ground – in fairness, often due to the pressures of modern political life. Certainly they have to avoid getting sucked into petty squabbling and to see things from a bigger perspective, but to do this they must show people on the ground that they are trusted. An argument must be presented to the members as advice, not an order. In fact, HQ must allow the membership to make the decision, confident that they will reach a fair conclusion. If they get it wrong, then they more than anyone else will have to live with the consequences.

Ned Reilly once told me that people will say all kinds of things and threaten to vote all kinds of ways, but given the responsibility when it comes down to the vote, people will do what they genuinely think is right for the Party. I agree with him on that score.

Ardagh were not impressed at losing out and threatened to dissolve the cumann for a while, so annoyed were they at the way it was handled. It is a dangerous practice to impose a candidate on a local organisation, and equally controversial when a candidate is added. However, it is also sometimes necessary. Conventions will often vote local, and select candidates without any regard to geography or numbers. Everyone at a convention has a view, and they stick to it, but there is a real danger that if you have several cumainn concentrated in one area, or who dislike a particular candidate, they may 'work' the convention to ensure that candidate is not selected. If you are observing from headquarters and you see this happening to a sitting candidate, or someone who you know is going to poll well with the public, then it becomes necessary to add that candidate to the ticket. It's not a nice thing to have to do, but it is a failsafe for the Party. At this point, HQ needs to explain the situation a little more – how shall I put it – persuasively. It comes down to winning co-operation, rather than instigating conflict. There is enough of that in most political parties.

Cumainn will often vote local and 'work' a convention, as I've said, but in my view this often happens because they know HQ will add a candidate anyway. Let me give you an example. Suppose Joe Bloggs is a sitting TD, but John Doe and Mary Everyman are also looking to compete at convention. HQ may say that only two candidates will be run due to numbers and geography, and this may well make sense. The local party on the ground, however, may feel that three candidates should be run. This may not be a sensible strategy, but not all the arguments and figures may not be available to everyone.

In the absence of real debate and discussion of the issue, the convention takes place. I guarantee that the cumainn will select John Doe and Mary Everyman as the candidates, because they know that it will be embarrassing that Joe Bloggs TD was not selected and therefore HQ will be forced to add him to the ticket and run three candidates in the end. The cumainn know that if they had done as HQ wanted and selected Joe Bloggs and Mary Everyman, then John Doe would not have been added and only two candidates would be run.

HQ needs to meet and discuss local electoral strategy well in advance of convention, and cumainn need to know that the rules are the rules, that they are given their opportunity but once they make a decision it will be final. Put to them that way, Joe Bloggs TD will be selected, as the cumainn would not dare to be at fault for blocking him – but they will block him if they know HQ will change its mind on behalf of certain people, but not on behalf of others.

Selection decided in Ballymahon, Mark Casey was said to have a good shot at taking a seat in Lanesboro. I talked to him on the night of the convention and told him that, although I may have supported Barney, he was the candidate now, and he would have my total and complete support should he need it. That's what I believe in; even if your man doesn't win, you get out and back the guy who does. It's better to have someone from your own political view elected than an opponent who doesn't agree with you at all.

We got another sharp reminder of how other things were so much more important than politics, when Dad suffered another heart attack in April and had to have more stents put in his heart. We really thought we had lost him this time, and we were very worried that it should happen again so soon. But like the old Trojan warrior that he is, he recovered and got himself ready for the local elections. He wouldn't deny the Party his vote when the election was this close.

Fianna Fáil took a pasting in the local elections. It was depressing but not unexpected; gone were the heady days of 2002. Des Kelly failed to get a seat in Lucan, and I have to admit that I only managed to get out canvassing with him once in the entire campaign, so like many others I was partially to blame. We lost control of several councils. Fine Gael were back in business and the size of their party machine was there to be seen – their Dáil numbers might have been cut, but they still had presence on the ground. Ballymahon was no different. It ended up 4–2 again, the only change being the fact that Mick Cahill pipped John Nolan for the last seat, changing Fianna Fáil's personnel. John had had a tough time politically and personally, and although a great man and a fine councillor, it was not to be. He took it with immense dignity.

Mark Casey was interesting. He lost out also, even though he put in a strong showing, an outcome I put down to two reasons. First, as I have said, if you are a prospective councillor you need your home area; you must be able to count on your own polling box to be a strong victory. There were two boxes in Lanesboro, and Casey didn't win either. Secondly, he didn't get enough votes in the Fermoyle polling booth but I feared at the time that when he canvassed he hadn't involved the Fermoyle cumann enough. In both Cashel and Lanesboro there is always a dangerous assumption that the people in the Fermoyle area, straddling the two parishes, are no different from their own. It's a fatal mistake. They may not be a parish but people in the Fermoyle area are very sure of their identity as one independent of either parish, and rally around each other more than most. Nonetheless, Mark had at least set himself up with a good base and could look to the future with some confidence. Even though a candidate may lose an election, it is all part of the process, and Mark was young enough to build on his vote and will certainly be a contender in the future. Candidates learn more from elections they have lost than those they have won.

I use this as an example to the young hopeful. Win your own ballot box and make sure the people you canvass with know the area intimately. I know also that our problem is, and will continue to be, that next time out prospective candidates will talk about how close they came to taking a seat at the last election, when all they are really talking about is how close they came to edging out another Fianna Fáil candidate. If you have two sitting councillors or TDs, then the third candidate should not be gauged on how close they are to one of your own, but on how close they came to unseating the opposing party. In the case of Ballymahon, we weren't within an ass's roar of doing that. You need to look at increasing the Party's number of seats, not just swapping personnel; that's what putting the Party first is all about.

The Europeans were no better for us. We lost three MEPs, a terrible blow. We couldn't say that it was unexpected; the polls and the media had been screaming it for months. It was annoying all the same. We felt we never got a fair crack of the whip. We were even fed up listening to Charlie Bird and George Lee on RTE, calling the opposition weak and ineffectual, just because they wouldn't throw out the same line that the media did. We felt that they went to great lengths to be negative, even about positive developments in the economy Some of what they said flew in the face of what other recognised experts were saying, and I'm sure they were shrewd enough to realise that some Party members felt that they were pushing a specific agenda.

I actually felt sorry for the opposition, because some of them were still trying to be responsible. They did understand how things were, and only wanted to stick the boot in when something was genuinely wrong. That policy makes sense to me; it's in the interest of the nation. And if you hold your fire, you will have greater impact when a government does slip up, which they will inevitably.

Enda Kenny was now the leader of Fine Gael, and I must admit I admired the guy as much as I can admire a Blueshirt. Don't get me wrong, sometimes he says things that leave me foaming at the mouth. I could hate him at times. But, then, he wouldn't be doing his job if I didn't. However, he did lead Fine Gael back from the brink.

A man derided for having almost no ministerial experience of any significance, he showed skills in party management that Fine Gael had been missing for far too long. He did many things with dignity. He attacked over-spending, for example, but not in the ridiculous sensationalist way that Eddie Hobbs did it. His was a measured attack that would not come back to haunt him if he were in power. He did not run out to make a meal of the Corrib gas situation in Mayo; instead he did his job and tried to find a resolution. He resisted personal or snide remarks in the Dáil, proving himself far more of a statesman than new Labour leader Pat Rabbitte. He adhered to old traditions like respect for the dead, and respect for families and friends of politicians. In short, Enda Kenny has the potential to be the biggest danger Fianna Fáil has faced for some years. He was implementing a form of Tallaght Strategy without the fuss, while still well able to put a knife in the back of the government. Oh, yes, I wouldn't trust him as far as I could throw him, although at times I'd love to throw him a very long distance. Occasionally he slips into attack just for the sake of it, but all politicians do that. My respect for him stems from his being an able opponent, but that said, I still think he is misguided, unfortunate, and an economic disaster waiting to happen. Why? Because he's a Blueshirt! They are all a bit mad; it's in the genes. Something funny happened them when they signed that Treaty!

The one benefit of a summer election is that when you lose you can head off on holiday and forget about things. People move on more quickly. I got my first year exam results from the PRII and scored very well in all subjects, which convinced me that I had taken the correct decision and that I was studying an area for which I actually had an aptitude. Annette, though, had reached a critical stage with her back. It was getting progressively worse. Her GP sent her back to the consultant who looked at it again and pretty much said that there was nothing that could be done, but perhaps she could get a brace. This time I was with her. 'No,' I said, 'something has to be done. This simply cannot continue.' Annette explained that she couldn't go on, continually on painkillers and out of work. Eventually he suggested referring her to a neurologist, Ciarán Bolger in the Mater private hospital. 'Maybe he will do something with the nerve, I don't know. I'll get the file together and send him a letter in about a fortnight – then, of course, it depends on when he can fit you in.'

Annette broke down in floods of tears on the way home – she was totally defeated by this. I was furious. I dropped her at her mother's house and turned the car to head back to the GP. 'You can't,' Annette said, 'you don't have an appointment,' but I knew I didn't need one. Dr Feeney was the type of guy who knew that if I showed up like this it was not without good reason. When I arrived he called me in straight away, and was just as concerned as I was when I explained what had happened. He immediately said that he would refer her to Ciarán Bolger himself, explain the urgency of the situation personally, and it would be done that day.

In a matter of days, Annette received a call and an appointment date. I would not forget that day in a hurry. She went in to see Ciarán Bolger on her own and came out crying her eyes out. I thought, 'Oh, no, what now?' But she hugged me and explained that they were tears of sheer joy. She had explained the situation to Ciarán Bolger, saying that she was due to get married the following year and did not want to be wheeled up the aisle, and he laughed and said, 'Well, we can't have that.' Then, whipped out the MRI scan, he held it up looked at it and said, 'Ah, yes, I think we can fix that all right. You'll just need a few weeks recovery.' He could not have understood what it meant to her to hear someone say this so confidently and simply. She was given an appointment for the beginning of September and she was overjoyed.

I decided to celebrate by taking her to see her teenage idols, Metallica, in concert. She was a Metallica nut. I got tickets through P. J. Mara and the ever-obliging Mike Hogan, and Mike very kindly arranged passes to the VIP section for us too. At this stage of my life, probably the only way I can enjoy Metallica is by sitting on a comfy chair and sipping a glass of wine. Annette was rocking away, though, still knowing every lyric of every song. When Mike heard she was a Metallica fan he said, 'Jaysus, Johnny, someone like you marrying a Metallica fan? I mean, I've heard of yin and yang, but that's just priceless.'

The joy did not last long, I'm afraid; Annette began to feel sick and bloated all the time. Everything she ate upset her. She had pains in her stomach and in her chest, and this went on for weeks. One Friday, I got us a Chinese, and we were all set for a nice evening in, but after one or two bites Annette put the plate to one side and began to cry. I felt like crying myself. Why was it that, when it seemed like the back problem could be solved, she was now feeling sick all the time. Like a typical man I said, 'Is everything OK?' even though I could see that everything plainly wasn't. But when I got my head together I said, 'Come on, let's put some things in a bag, you're going to A&E.' After her experience in Beaumont she was resistant, but I can be fairly forceful when I want. I put it simply. 'Nothing minor can cause that much pain. There has to be something seriously wrong.' We stopped at her Mam's house and Rachael helped to convince her that going to hospital was the right thing to do. When we got out of the car at Tallaght, Annette was still fuming that we were making her do this. 'This is stupid, I'm going in here to be treated like shite and told all I need is to let out a bloody big fart.' Ah, always the lady!

Tallaght was a very different experience, though, and I cannot speak highly enough of the medical staff there. Despite how busy the hospital was, we were only waiting an hour for her to be seen. At first, they thought of things like irritable bowel syndrome and Crohn's disease, but as time went on it became something very different. They started talking about her womb and her ovaries, and mentioning something called endometriosis. Man, that was a name for a disease, and would certainly be one for the old first class spelling test, right up there with the dreaded 'Salmon of Knowedge'. Apparently a huge proportion of women have this but as most cases are mild the majority of people have never even heard of it. Annette couldn't understand how it could cause symptoms like chest pains, but when I consulted my trusty old friend the Internet, I could see that this bloody disease can cause practically anything. It's like an Alien, in fact you could make a bloody good film out of it! It grows inside women, strangling their ovaries and womb, latches on to other organs, sticking them together, and it is created by the menstrual cycle so you can't get rid of it until you can no longer have kids. The only ongoing treatment is to be on the pill. Without the pill, it grows wild. And here were we thinking that the pill was bad for you. That's science for ya, they prove one thing only to disprove it with something else they prove. Scientists are in a continual race against themselves.

Annette had to undergo a series of operations to solve this problem. The final operation fell close to a holiday we had planned in Gran Canaria, but the doctors felt the operation was a great success and allowed her travel, with the usual caveats about not doing anything strenuous. No problems there, we intended lying in the sun and taking things very easy.

Annette's parents, Martin and Rachael, went too, though they stayed in another resort. We used to visit them and then head out for a meal and stuff. We certainly made the most of the rest time; in fact the holiday itself was very relaxing. There was also a great pub called the Nineteenth Hole, and we had great sport up there, singing along as you do after a few pints. We even did karaoke, which was wonderful fun, and something Annette would never ever try at home. I just did the reliable old Joe Dolan number for my stint at the microphone.

Annette wasn't feeling the best, though, and the next day she was in bits. She was in bed, burning up, in real pain and drifting between talking normally and talking total nonsense. I ran out to the front desk and rang a doctor. 'Oh, no, no, there is something very wrong here, senor,' she said, the moment she arrived. She called an ambulance straight away, and Annette was wheeled out on a trolley, past all the shocked-looking people in the pool. When she got to the hospital, they did everything they could for her. The scans showed there was an internal bleed somewhere.

Annette struggled through the flight back the following Saturday, and was in a right state by the time we landed at Dublin. We got her in a taxi and made straight for the hospital. She was operated on again and again as they tried to solve the problem. Apparently the strain of 'endo' was particularly aggressive, and though the original operation should have left her clear for some time, in her case it came back worse than ever, and after only a couple of weeks it had grown back all over the shop again. Because of this, her back operation had to be postponed until October. But, more than anything, the news of the illness affected us both deeply because it meant that conceiving a baby could be difficult. I guess you never realise how much you would like to have kids until someone tells you that you might not be able. It wasn't a priority, but it was something we had always assumed would happen. Annette was heartbroken.

With Annette being so ill, we had to miss another great moment: Longford Town winning the League cup. I hadn't even got to many matches with everything that had been happening over the summer, but it was great to see the club take another trophy. Nothing for years, then suddenly two senior trophies within twelve months. God is good, even if he doesn't always play a blinder.

Annette finally got to have her back operation, and although she was laid up for weeks and couldn't climb stairs, the operation was a success and her recovery was good. She will always have to be careful with her back, but Ciaran Bolger deserves a medal for the job he did. It was amazing to see Annette so optimistic and happy again. The recovery was tough, but it was well worth it.

Fianna Fáil's reaction to the Party's losses in the local and European elections was to be expected: there was a cabinet re-shuffle. These are strange things indeed. They create great excitement, but must be a total pain for any minister involved. They are not something we are particularly accustomed to in Ireland, and it was rumoured that this one would be pretty extensive. In the end, the big news was that McCreevy went to Brussels and Cowen took over at Finance, leaving him well positioned for leadership, having held both the main economic and social portfolios. Mícheál Martin got out of the department of health and went to enterprise and employment, which he needed to do as he had not yet held an economic ministry, and it's a pre-requisite if you are to be a Fianna Fáil leader. Noel Dempsey was unfortunate to be moved out of education, which needs someone willing to think outside the box and who is not afraid to face down vested interests or drag people, if needs be kicking and screaming, into a new era. But he was quite happy once he got to communications, marine and natural resources, a department with much greater scope and a far more progressive outlook than the old stodgy halls of education.

Mary Hanafin moved into education. That was a good move, a good place to start her first ministry. It's not the most important department in the country but it is one of the most difficult to handle. Séamus Brennan was gutted when he had to move to social welfare; he is an economic rather than social thinker. Although I have great admiration for his abilities, he has been at the cutting edge of politics since the days of Jack Lynch, something not many people can say; and even though he still has much to offer, personally I always thought he was the ideal man for Europe. But McCreevy had gone there, and although he would be missed there was a chance for new ideas to come to the fore. Amazingly, PD leader Mary Harney took health. Was she mad? In a word, yes.

The problem in health is that the politicians can't get agreement among themselves. We need a strong minister who is not interested in claiming a prize for him or her self. It is clear that, when trying to sort out problems in that department, a number of groups are just not going to help. First, the Department of Health in its own right. It's not in control, spending is gone out of its claws, it ends up overseeing waste and trying to justify it. Second, health management. Management is the last thing that happens; the managers have no control over central functions of hospitals such as beds and resources, other than getting new ones. And then there are consultants. Don't get me started – they are wonderful medical people, but that does not qualify them in knowing how to manage people, resources or, most crucially, hospital accommodation. It would be the same as me turning around and saying that, because I earn a few fees for my company in my chosen field, I should be in control of finances, even though I have no expertise in that area. Madness. Finally, nurses. Yes, indeed; those poor souls who wander around in dark corridors with candle wax dripping on their freezing hands, living saints who are paid nothing but do what they do out of sheer concern for patients. Give me a break. Yes, they do a fine job, but they are no different to any other sector of our economy. They want top pay, extra allowances, all the usual public sector perks. It means nothing that there is no money to pay for it, though the government could stop spending it on a sports hall or some other useful service, and put it in nurses salaries instead.

Apologies to all the nurses who, as you saw earlier, I greatly admire. But they can't solve the problem either, and, unfortunately, when an issue reaches the point of crisis that the health service has reached, there is no room for sentiment. Tough talk and action needs to be taken, however harsh that may seem. It is only natural that various interests look out for themselves and their own concerns, and once we accept that and are up-front about it we can begin to deal with their suggestions in a more productive fashion. There is no point in each of these groups blaming the government or any particular minister when they themselves are unwilling to change.

We need a minister to call together all health spokespersons in the Dáil and have them agree to a plan, and agree they will stand by it. This should be an Oireachtas initiative in the interest of the nation. The same kind of all-party consensus that existed in relation to Northern Ireland. With that, politicians can face down the strikes, do what is necessary to stop the sheer madness of wasted money, and then they can all claim a piece of the credit at the election. Sure, they will consult with everyone and anyone to get a full brief, but they must take the tough decisions together. Painful but necessary. The only people who can sort out the problems in health are people who are not connected with it for a living. Those who have nothing to gain must do it. And it must be in the interests of the patient.

Things looked up for the government after the reshuffle. It was a chance to re-invigorate the Party, to get a new atmosphere in government. Politics is all about perception and sometimes a change in personnel can bring in new ideas that help to display you in a different light. I know people will say that is shallow, but it really is just further evidence that politics is more to do with who you trust than anything else. I believe passionately in the political system. It does have its faults and is far from perfect; yes, there are loopholes and ways of corrupting the system. But no other system allows all of the people to take part in the process. It is not exclusive and we all have a choice to be as involved as we want in any political party.

Politics is certainly not easy, you can find it incredibly frustrating at times, yet it remains the only avenue for true, fair and lasting change in society. It is not built on fear or strength, but on beliefs. Our political parties debate issues, our politicians are some of the most accessible in the world. The process may be slow – it can often take years to convince people of the rightness of your view, and have that taken on board at a Party level, but that is simply because everyone else is afforded their right to argue the toss with you. Politics is not a quick fix like revolution; it will not solve all problems overnight, but at least, when it does something, it lasts.

One of the only problems in society today is the failure to get ordinary people engaged in politics to the same degree as they were before. It is true that politicians have done themselves no favours, but despite that they remain the only part of our society that is completely answerable to the people. The man in the street cannot decide who looks after planning decisions or who works at what in the council; they remain faceless. The man in the street has no say in what people control the decision-making process in the civil service.

The man in the street most certainly has no control over the media or those who comment on the news. However, you do get to decide who will represent you in government.

Unfortunately, in recent times people have been convinced that politicians cannot be trusted, that they 'are all the same' and that they are worthy of nothing but disdain. The ironic thing is that this viewpoint is leading on a path where power can be gradually removed from politicians to non-elected individuals; in other words, the power is being removed from the people. The media have played a large part in this, to the point where people are now convinced that what political parties say is just propaganda, but what is said in the media must be gospel. They say the greatest trick the devil ever played was to convince the world that he did not exist. The greatest trick the media have ever played was in convincing people that politicians cannot be trusted.

Politics is a lot like football in many ways. Everybody is out there supporting their team, sitting in pubs arguing the strengths and weaknesses of the teams, and debating the merits of particular players and selections. In the run up to a general election we are in a sort of 'closed season', waiting for the premiership to begin. As always, at this point everyone thinks they can win the championship. Ok, we all know that everyone really wants to associate themselves with Liverpool or Manchester United but that is because of their history and support and if you take both of those teams out then I reckon the next election is shaping up very much like next seasons premiership:

Fianna Fáil are Chelsea, lots of money, all the big name players, coming off back to back titles and looking for a historic three in a row, but very unpopular at the moment and everyone wants to see them toppled. They need to find some more excitement in attack if they are to win back public opinion.

Fine Gael are Arsenal. They have managed to shed the 'boring' tag in recent years, have some top class players but need the entire squad to perform better and do so on a more consistent basis. They have won titles in the past but after a very bad showing last time out that left them well off the pace, they need to be challenging for the title this time.

Labour are Newcastle. They look very good when attacking but are still suspect in defence. They score some great goals but this is offset by an inability to defend their position. We know it is highly unlikely that they will win the championship themselves next time out but they could have a significant bearing on who does win it, especially if they can up their game against Chelsea, but don't be surprised if right at the end of the campaign they end up helping Chelsea to the title either.

Progressive Democrats are Wigan Athletic. Not the biggest of teams however last time out they surprised all their critics and did much better than expected, putting themselves among the big boys. However next year is going to be a very big test to see if they can maintain that position and emulate their last performance.

Sinn Féin are Celtic, most SF supporters will be happy with this analogy, but the reason I make it is that while they are a good side and can play an attractive game, no one wants to play in the same league as them and therefore they cannot win the premiership. So, instead they have their own separate goals to achieve. There is no doubt that they want to play in the premiership though and are making efforts to be admitted, it may happen in the near future but not this season.

The Green Party are Reading. A good performance in their last league outing means they have earned the right to play with the big teams. They will be an unknown quantity and might hit great heights or slip to a difficult defeat. Lots of potential but are probably going to be asked a lot more searching questions next season and will have to be able to defend in depth.

Independents are like Watford. Who knows what they will be like? Will they be like Wigan last season and have a big influence on things especially in the early stages or will they disappear into oblivion like Sunderland ...

14

TO INFINITY AND BEYOND

Would you believe it? Longford town was in the final of another FAI cup. This was the stuff of pure fantasy.

This time there was no doubt in Annette's mind that she was going to the match. We went out on the Saturday night with Annette's friends and some of mine from work, and Pádraig Loughrey came up to stay with us for the game. I drank far too much, including a fat frog, and it made me violently ill that night, so Annette was far from impressed, but you can't argue on cup final day, and we met up with Margarita and Kenneth at our place and got a bus into town. Last year, Kenneth left at the last minute, and left an unimpressed Margarita behind, so to make up for it he said he would bring her and foot the bill next time Longford made it – he had no idea that would be the very next year.

It was a great feeling, all heading off in our scarves and flags, taking over the city again. In and around Lansdowne was full of the same old how-are-you-doing, but it was getting like an annual trip to Dublin at this stage. When we got into the ground, though, the atmosphere was very different. Waterford just didn't bring much of a crowd, for such a big city and club, and were easily outnumbered by the Longford fans. And there wasn't the same banter as with the Pat's crowd; on the contrary, it seemed openly hostile. Five Waterford bucks sat down in the very front section of the East stand, in front of all the Longford fans. They had too much to drink and were abusive to girls and even children that passed, throwing stuff and jeering at them, so much so that people were afraid to pass by. They continually jeered and goaded the Longford fans, who to their credit did not respond.

Longford were brutal, right from the start. This year it was us who just weren't showing up. The atmosphere among the fans wasn't made much better by the knowledge that the Waterford manager Alan Reynolds, had once spent a season with Town. It was nil–nil at half time and not a sign of Town making a decent move. Annette looked at me and said, 'It's just not the same as last year. There's no fun at all, and those five fellas down the front are really pissing me off. I wish Longford would score just to stuff it to them.' I laughed. Go on, the Dub!

So, second half: disaster. Waterford get a break down the left and, bang, it's 1–0. Stunned to silence. A feeling like your stomach has just dropped to your feet. Longford looking lost.

But, afterwards, Graham Gartland, who was Longford centre half that day, as we were without captain Barry Ferguson, said that shortly after the Waterford goal, when it was their fans who should have been singing, the entire east stand stood up chanting, 'Stand up if you're Longford town'. At that moment, the players knew they had to do something.

Longford improved but were still not looking like scoring. Seven minutes to go and I turned to Annette and said, 'Sorry, love, it just doesn't look like it's going to be our day. We can't have it every year, I guess.'

Five minutes to go, the ball breaks to Alan Kirby, the former Waterford player. He jinks, then takes a step forward and drives it. Oh my God! Longford have levelled right at the death.

The crowd went wild. The five Waterford fans held their head in their hands as the Longford fans waved down at them. We were all jumping across each other. Annette was crying with delight as she hugged me, and the crowd kept cheering for an eternity, the longest goal cheer I can ever remember. It was pure joy; we would have a replay and then we would perform better, live to fight again.

We were just started into another round of 'Stand up if you're Longford Town' when suddenly, only two minutes since the goal, the ball falls to Paul Keegan, the striker who had not scored for the entire season so far, and yes, he stuck it in the net! The roar was deafening. Fans jumped the barriers. Even the team ran about like crazy men. The Longford fans now wreaked revenge, swarming the partition surrounding the five Waterford boys and wrapping red and black flags around them, and they started to cry. I roared until my throat could take no more, then felt tears run down my cheek.

'Champione, champione are we.'

I heard afterwards of a Waterford fan who left with five minutes to go to get to his car, beat the traffic home, and get a good spot for the celebration in Waterford. By the time he had turned on his radio, Longford Town were lifting the cup. It was the most extraordinary come back. Annette looked at me after returning from the barrier where she threw all kinds of abuse and gestures at those five Waterford fans, and said, 'Ah, yes, this is more like it. This is the best feeling ever.'

Seeing Longford Town lift the cup for the second year running was surreal. It was a moment to savour for the rest of our lives. We talked about those couple of minutes for the rest of the night, replaying every single detail, as we had a Chinese and rather a lot of alcohol with Margarita and Kenneth.

It's difficult to explain to people our unique pride. Longford is a small county. We haven't ever won much, outside of the Leinster title in 1968, the national league in 1966, the FAI cup in 2003, the league cup in 2004 and the FAI cup again in 2004. Actually, when it's put like that, we haven't done too badly for a population no bigger than Lucan. I remember visiting a mate of mine, Gerry McEvoy, who lived with a number of Cork lads while he was in DCU, including the hurler Seán Óg Ó hAilpín. Myself and a couple of other lads dropped over, and by the time we left the Cork fellas agreed on one thing.

'Jaysus, boy, I never met a group of lads so proud of their county, and what's worse is ye have no fuckin' right to be!'

They were right in one way but wrong in another. People talk about Leitrim and Cavan, but at least everyone knows of them, even if it is just to slag them. On school trips we used to play a game with people where we would give them thirty-two guesses to discover which county we were from, and very few ever got it. You could be sure they would name some county twice before they ever got around to Longford. Annette taught kids at school who asked her what county Longford was in.

But I also remember coming home on the train one weekend, waiting at the door of the carriage as the train pulled in, and two lads in front of me who were also about to get out said, looking at the lights of the town, 'Ah, all the same, it's a great auld place, Longford, isn't it?' That pretty much sums it up for us Longfordians. We are insulated from the outside world; things are only important if they affect us. We have an extreme passion and pride, even if by other people's standards they think we have nothing to be proud of. In a sense, it's not trophies or buildings or any of that stuff that we are proud of, it's just we ourselves, the people and the craic.

People always tell you that when you are getting married the time will just fly by. Well, they are not lying. Everything takes a back seat to the plans, although we were pretty well organised thanks to the fact that we had prepared well in advance. In the meantime, I secured my dream move work wise, and had been appointed government affairs analyst at A&L Goodbody Consulting. Unfortunately, I moved to the consultancy wing just as one of my best friends there, Declan Byrne, was about to leave. Declan had been instrumental in helping me prepare for interviews and I found his advice invaluable. He went on to set up his own consultancy firm, Byrne Conroy. We meet up for the occasional pint to talk about work, politics, football and life. Declan is the kind of friend you need if you want to stay cool, a guy who could wear pink and get away with it. Not many could, could they?

I was finally getting the opportunity to put my knowledge of politics and my contacts across all parties to good use. People sometimes ask me, 'What happens if the other guys take power?' to which the answer is, of course, that for me nothing changes. That's the thing about government and public affairs. If you look at all the main players, they were all politically connected: P. J. Mara (FF)

Nuala Fennell (FG), Niall Ó Muilleoir (FG), Martin Mackin (FF) – the list goes on. The thing about it is that, if you are going to be effective in this area, it is desirable, if not wholly necessary, to have been involved in politics. Why? Because politicians need to know that whoever is coming to them understands their position, can help them overcome problems at their end, and is politically aware. If a Fianna Fáil minister is approached by a government affairs expert with a Fine Gael background, then the minister knows, first of all, where the consultant is coming from. The minister knows that the consultant's reputation depends on treating him fairly, and he knows that the consultant understands politics and the problems he faces as a minister – and can help resolve them.

Lobbying and the public affairs area has come in for some very bad press recently. Most of that is down to one man, Frank Dunlop. Ah, Frank, you had to go and make an arse of things. Recent tribunals uncovered the fact that Dunlop bribed several councillors in the Dublin area to have lands zoned for development. These developments were for the benefit of his clients. There is no way around it: no party or group can make any excuse for what Frank Dunlop did. In one sense a person might be able to make up a sob story for some councillors, along the lines of hard times, high election expenses, no remuneration of any worth for councillors at the time, mounting debts, lands that would have had to have been rezoned eventually anyway, so when they had a chance of taking a few bob they did. Well that's the kind of excuse you could make up anyway if you were trying to understand it, although you cannot get away from the fact that it was downright wrong and how any councillor could not see it was plainly wrong is beyond me. Don't get me wrong I am not making any excuse for those councillors here, I am more annoyed than most at them for the damage they did to our political system. The reason I make the point though is to show just how completely impossible the situation with Frank Dunlop was. He was giving the money, he had no overheads or election expenses, he knew what he was doing was corrupt, and he went right ahead. He showed no regard for politics, party, good name or friends. It was purely personal gain and there was no way it could be described as anything else.

Is lobbying different today? Well, it's different from the Frank Dunlop school, that's for sure. In fact, it seems to me that Frank Dunlop knew very little about lobbying at all, really. Any true professional in this game knows it's about looking at a case, stripping out the bits that might be unworkable, and trying to match it to a public need. It's about finding solutions that benefit the government, the public and the client.

Lobbying usually involves a company that has an idea, a way of doing something more efficiently, and needs to convince the government that their solution can work effectively. That's what lobbying is. Nothing corrupt, nothing underhand, and in fact something that benefits the public immensely. Many private companies have great ideas, but they don't understand politics. They have elements which politicians don't like or which go against policy, or else their plans do not incorporate basic tenets of government thinking. It's the lobbyist's job to merge the two and bring forward a proposal to solve the problem. Lobbyists are a vital link between government and the private sector, and provide a great service to the state. The public generally doesn't recognise this, and that's down to those smart-arses in the media, who grew up on dope-fuelled conspiracy theories in the '60s and '70s and haven't the good sense to realise that a lot of people just want to do what is right.

Annette and I set a date for 18 June, and the last few weeks were hectic. I must admit that the bride does do most of the work. Annette wrote all the invitations, arranged the flowers, did everything, really. I got the mass booklets done at work, which was handy, and Ciaran McGuinness, who was to be my groomsman, helped us pick some nice tunes. Ciaran was going to play the flute, and another good friend, Emer Barry, agreed to be the soloist. We were thrilled to have them. Emer is the finest singer of her generation, and opera fans are bound to see her name in lights very soon.

As groom, my main task was to look after myself and make sure I made it to the altar in one piece. This was one of Annette's biggest fears, because I played football every Friday with some of the partners and solicitors at work. It was a great way to keep fit, even if the rivalry between two of the partners, Mark Ward and John Coman, often heated up the game. Other solicitors, like Karl Henson, Dennis Agnew and Lee Murphy, had a real desire to win, too. I was a lot smaller than most of them, but I reckoned I could avoid serious injury. Politics had never allowed me the time to cultivate my footballing career, but the occasional appearance in serious games over the years had convinced me that it was all about trying. Annette was worried that I'd try too hard and end up with a black eye or broken leg for the big day.

My stag party down in Laois did nothing to allay her fears. We went Paintballing. I would recommend it to anyone. It's like being five years old again, only this time you can get hurt. Playing war games in a forest, running through the mud shooting enemies all over the shop. Playing the hero and running at the enemy, only to be cut down. There I was, just like Pádraig Pearse and Wolfe Tone, giving my all for the cause. And it bloody hurts when you are shot. We arrived home with cuts on our heads and hands, and bruises all over our bodies – the womenfolk looked shocked when we came through the door. We were as happy as little kids, rushing to tell them our war stories and the tactical and strategic details of our battles and heroics.

I changed the car once more. This time I upgraded to an '04 Peugeot 307. For most guys, the type of car they drive signifies the stage of life they are at. I had a reasonably good and new car now, so obviously I was doing OK career wise. I bought a car that was in the sexy-styling bracket, so evidently I still fancied myself a bit. And I bought a family car that had all the safety features and lots of room; that was something to think about, too.

I used to always wonder what it would be like to get married, what were the nerves that everyone talked about. Well, I can safely say it was the greatest day of my life, the most amazing thing I have ever done. The night before the wedding, Mick and Ciaran stayed at our house, while Annette went back to her mother's. Funnily enough, when you're getting married you nearly forget that you have to go on honeymoon afterwards. This meant that Annette, when she was leaving to go to her Mam's, not only had to get everything she needed together for the wedding, but also to pack for a three-week holiday. That was probably the most stressful part for her. Being a bloke, my packing took about fifteen minutes – lift clothes out of drawer into case.

Once Annette and the women had all gone, we – the lads, that is – could start to relax, after all the panic and talk about the big day. We sat for a while reminiscing about the old days at St Mel's, and how mad it was that one of us was finally getting married. This day used to seem very far away when we were wandering up the avenue to school, talking about the girls we were into or had shifted, and who was going with whom. Then we ordered a Domino's pizza and sat watching a ridiculous programme on television about a gang of bikers in New Zealand who were totally anti-establishment, broke every law they could, and tattooed themselves all over. Yeah, I'd say their lives were a lot of fun all right. After some more chat we decided that we had best get to bed – we had an early start in the morning. The lads agreed fairly readily, and I was delighted because I intended going up to the room to practice the old speech. When I got upstairs, I could hear Mick practising his speech next door, while Ciaran was knocking out a few notes on the flute downstairs. So, we had the same idea anyway.

The next morning I think the two lads were more nervous than me. We got up early, headed into the city centre, and went for breakfast in Bewleys, which is a great spot since it was taken over by Café Bar Deli – Jay Bourke is a good friend of mine, and it's always a good thing to support a friend in any way you can. After a hearty feed in Bewleys, we had some time to waste, and took a walk around Stephen's Greens. We were so laid back at this stage we were horizontal. The last time the three of us had been together here was when we were busking on Grafton Street as teenagers. We took a break and lay down in the Green, where a guy approached us offering strawberries and other fruits, although he had no visible signs of having any fruit on him whatsoever. Then he went a bit foolish, talking about whiz, but we had already gone to the jacks, and I couldn't see what business it was of his anyway. Eventually he asked me if any of us were on trips.

'Ah, sure,' says I confidently, 'we're all up from Longford for the day.'

We laughed about it now, being a lot older and wiser. After a stroll around the Green, we headed into the Grafton barber for some hot towel shaves. These are not for the faint-hearted. You feel like you are going to smother, or at lest be scalded beyond all recognition, when they put those progressively hotter towels on your face. They also gave me a cigar and a glass of brandy beforehand. I duly knocked back the brandy, only to be told by the barber, 'You shouldn't drink before you're shaved. The alcohol thins the blood, so you bleed more.' Now he tells me.

I got quite a fright when he turned me to the mirror after the shave; my face was covered in blood, it was streaming from several nicks. Oh, fuck, I thought, Annette is going to fuckin' kill me. I am so dead. Of all the bloody days!

The barber told me to relax and got to work putting oil on the little nicks, and they all disappeared like magic. When he was finished, I looked right as rain. Oh, Lord, me heart. To be honest, I wasn't nervous about getting married at all; what made me nervous was looking right for Annette when she walked up the church. Today was the one day more than any when I wanted her opinion. I wished I could turn around and say, 'Do I look OK?' But of course I couldn't, not in church. If it weren't for the fact that I knew she would be up to her tonsils, I would have sent her a picture on the phone to get her opinion, but I couldn't do that either.

We went back to the house and got into the suits. Time started to speed up now. Mick was in a right state about his speech, and told me he wanted me to speak after him, they way we used to at debates, otherwise he was afraid his speech would not look as good. I knew he was worrying about nothing but I agreed. Ciaran was taking every moment he could to run over the tunes he had to play. We got in the car eventually, all blokish backslapping and camaraderie, and headed for the church. We had only arrived when we met Margarita and Kenneth, who were the first there. Lucky thing, too, because we couldn't get the flowers into our jackets and Margarita sorted it out for us. We made our way into the church, and Emer and Ciaran got set up for the music. I paced around the place like a guard outside Buckingham Palace on ecstasy. I wasn't nervous about Annette not showing up, but I was nervous that anything should go wrong. I wouldn't be truly comfortable until I was making my speech.

Gradually the crowd started to make their way in, everyone saying hello to me, which was great but also like I was on show. Peter Kelly, TD, who was bringing Annette to the church, and my cousin Bernard Woods, had gone to collect the ladies, so I decided that there was nothing for it but to go to my seat, sit down and wait. What I didn't know was that Annette and Peter had to turn back because they forgot the rings, but eventually we could hear the commotion as they arrived.

Now, this bit is difficult for the groom. Annette had imposed a rule that I wasn't to look around until she was beside me, which meant that while everyone in the church was looking around, I had to stand with my eyes glued to the crucifix. The urge to turn was almost unbearable. Then the music kicked off, and I relaxed.

Annette looked amazing. That's the only word I can find for it. It is indescribable how I felt looking at her; I was happier than I had ever been before. The ceremony went perfectly, which spoke volumes for Annette's planning skills. The celebrant, Fr Moore, took plenty of opportunity, being a Dub, to lay into Longford and the culchies. He was quite hard on us, but I didn't mind, I knew

I'd have right of reply in my speech at the dinner. Then came the photographs, a tough business, standing for ages posing this way and that, the muscles in your jaws aching from smiling. I can tell you, I totally understand the model who said she wouldn't get out of bed for less than £10,000. She was right. If your job was that boring and tiring, you would want a hell of a lot of money to do it.

We were led into the reception by a piper, and eventually sat down for the meal. Ciaran was in a state about reading the telegrams, and Mick and I were in a state about making our speeches. You want so much for it to be good, for people to enjoy it, that you get nervous. I am always nervous until I start to speak, and then I find it's the one place I am truly at home. I was born for that; I know it. Once I start making a speech, I'm more comfortable than doing anything else.

In the end, it all went swimmingly; all the speeches were fantastic. Annette was afraid for her Dad because he is deaf, and she thought it might be tough for him to get up and speak, but he was brilliant on the day and was well able to embarrass Annette with a few stories from her childhood. My Dad was phenomenal too, with a speech that had everyone in tears. One of the highlights was his recounting how he had come to Dublin thirty years before and found a wife. 'It's a good thing to marry a Dub,' he concluded. I couldn't agree more.

Mick was great as well; no messing, no smutty jokes that so many best men descend to, just the truth about what kind of mates we are and some of the things we did. I was really honoured to have him as my best man on the day and to realise that he really did think highly of me.

Unfortunately, Albert and Kathleen Reynolds couldn't be there on the day, but they sent a nice telegram and a more than generous present. Noel and Bernadette Dempsey came along with their daughter, Aileen, and her boyfriend, Ronan. I was delighted they were able to make it, as they are such good friends and great people, too. Peter Kelly was snapping photographs like he had just got a contract for Hello magazine. My relations Jan, Juan and Clara came all the way from Spain. There was no doubt, though, that it was a political wedding – even Bertie Ahern sent a telegram, which was greeted with the awe due to a Fianna Fáil leader.

It was a wonderful gathering and the most fun either Annette or I had ever had. The only thing that was difficult was getting to talk to everyone. In the end, we decided that the best thing we could do was to get out on the dance-floor, and we danced until our legs couldn't hold us up any more.

It was nearly daybreak by the time Annette and I flopped across the bed and fell into a deep, deep sleep. We were staying another night in the hotel, which gave us time to meet our wedding guests again, especially all my neighbours from Longford, whom I saw all too rarely for my liking. On Monday, we flew to Rome, where we were going to stay for a week, and then spend two weeks in Sorrento.

Rome was amazing on so many levels. Sometimes just sitting in Giovanni's Trattoria, eating good food and enjoying a nice wine. Other times it was wandering through the forum, walking where men like Caesar and Pompey walked, touching the stones from which western civilisation emanated. Wondering in awe at the achievements of the Romans, who lasted for far longer than any other civilisation. America, Britain, France, Germany, the EU, are all only in the ha'penny place by comparison. Yet they are all the inheritors of Rome and its ways. The ideals of the EU are often scarily close to the ideals of the Romans, without the warfare, of course. When you stand in the coliseum, you are horrified, awestruck and proud all at once. We may have lost the passion for death, but we are all still Romans when it comes down to it.

And as a Catholic visiting home of the church, it felt astounding to see the crib Christ was born in, the pillar at which he was flogged, pieces of the true cross and the steps from Pontius Pilate's house which he walked down when he was condemned. The Vatican, the cathedrals and churches, the museums; it was all here.

We went for an audience with the pope, which involved waiting in St Peter's Square from 9 a.m. until 11 a.m. before the hour-long audience began. This is Rome in summer, and you are like an egg on a frying-pan sitting there, it really is a penance. By the time the pope comes out, to a greeting that would leave a rock star jealous, you are already exhausted. Then he talks about psalm 129. Ok, not very exciting stuff, but, hey, he has to say everything in seven languages, which really makes you wish that the church had stuck to Latin. Then he must acknowledge all the people and groups who want to be welcomed, and calls out their names. If you are a group going to Rome, please don't do this, I'm begging you. It may be wildly exciting for your group for the two seconds it takes to read your name, everyone else is tired and bored, and no one remembers you afterwards anyway. The poor pope must get fed-up of having to sit through it, too, and he can't very well throw a hissy fit and say he's not doing it. No, the poor pope has to love everyone.

While we were still in Rome I got a text to tell me that the PR diploma exam results were out. Annette rang her brother, Damien, who was house sitting for us, and told him to open the envelope, as I waited anxiously, butterflies all over. Annette called out the results one by one, and by the time she reached the end of it, I was dancing around the balcony. College was finally over! Passing exams is one of the best feelings, and you just have to celebrate. To put in so much work and finally see it pay off is just magic. That's what Annette told me anyway, because up to this point I had never experienced anything other than keeping my head above water. She was right though; it is worth it.

Sorrento was more relaxed than the buzzing city of Rome, sitting every night enjoying a meal and wine looking out over the Bay of Naples and Mount Vesuvius. The city of Pompeii was an amazing sight, even if it was tough work trudging around the streets in the heat. Herculaneum is easier to navigate, and I would even say more interesting, as the place is more intact, the blackened, burned timbers a permanent reminder of that horrific day. Vesuvius is due another eruption; a scary thought.

It was an amazing holiday, sitting chatting late into the hot Italian nights with my wife. There was never a time I felt more content. I thought about my life a lot in those few weeks, and I was in no doubt that I had done ok for myself. I had a job I loved that involved politics. I had a beautiful wife. And, in fairness to myself, I had come a long way. It seemed a million years since those pre-election bashes in the Peer Inn, since Albert had become Taoiseach, since people used to talk about me being a guy meant for great things in politics. Yet it had all passed like the blink of an eye. Here I was, nearly thirty, no longer could I claim to impress people by what I knew 'at such a young age'. Now it was expected of me. I thought of all the good times I had had, and I knew that if I had it over, I wouldn't change a single thing. I thought of all the smart-arses, too, and felt I could forgive them their inability to see. We would never be rid of them anyway – poor old Scipio, Pompey and Caesar experienced the same problems.

So this book is, in truth, all about growing up, and growing up in a great political party in a country to be proud of. We truly do have a great country. And that's not down to ideologies; they gave Ireland nothing. It's not down to the media, which has brought it more pain than help. It's not down to experts who claim to be a-political. It's down to the hard work and graft of the common people. More than anything, it's down to the people who took part in the democratic process. Those who selected and elected the men and women of all parties and shades of political opinion who made our country and supported them through thick and thin. To all those people who keep political parties going by volunteering, it may seem a thankless task, but you are the people who give us democracy.

As I gazed upon the ruins of the Forum Romanum, the words inscribed on the foundation stone of Leinster House kept running through my head. 'Hence learn, when in some unhappy day, you light upon the ruins of so great a mansion, of what worth he was who built it, and how frail all things are, when such memorials of such men, cannot outlive misfortune.' May we never light upon the ruins of Leinster House, or all is truly lost.

So I sat with my wife as the sun descended beyond the Bay of Naples, holding her hand and thinking of how swiftly it had all changed for the once mighty Romans. Well Johnny boy, I thought, you couldn't have given it any more so far. Who knows what the future holds; maybe I will be Taoiseach. Maybe I will end my days as a public affairs consultant. I might even become a well-known author who crops up on Questions and Answers from time to time.

I know that, whatever happens, once I have Annette, my family and my friends, I will be happy. Even if it were all to end tomorrow, I wouldn't go with a frown on my face, but with a great big smile. I've had a ball. So let's finish off that bottle of wine and see what the future brings. And in the best traditions of the Party; 'fuck the begrudgers.'

ACKNOWLEDGMENTS

At the end of a project like this book its always nice to sit down with a glass of wine and try to recall all the people you should thank. I am indebted to Mary Feehan at Mercier Press for seeing some potential in a very rough manuscript. To Patrick, Catherine, Brian and all at Mercier for their help; I couldn't have asked for more supportive or better publishers.

To P. J. Mara for reading the manuscript and writing the fore-word; you will always be a legend. To Albert Reynolds and the Reynolds family, without all of your friendship this book, like so much else in my life, would not have happened. To all those involved in Fianna Fáil in Longford, Dundalk and Dublin, you taught me so much and I have been privileged to know and work with such fine people. To all the members of Fianna Fáil across the country, you never cease to amaze me.

To the opponents I met along the way from all parties, if you weren't so good I would have learned nothing. A special thank you to Derek Union for taking the author photograph. To Margarita and Kenneth, you guys are more important to me than you realise, - thank you. To Mam and Dad for introducing me to politics, for bringing me up and supporting me in everything I have ever done, I can never repay you. Finally to Annette, for putting up with all the politics, for believing in me, for reading the first draft and encouraging me, for watching me down many bottles of wine and listening to me pontificate, for showing me that there is always more to life than you think and most of all for being my wife.

Con Cremin
Ireland's Wartime Diplomat

Dr Niall Keogh

ISBN: 1 85635 497 0

Paris, 1939. A hazardous place to begin a diplomatic career, but the first in a series of vital postings for the young Con Cremin, who observed history unfolding in a continent dominated by Adolf Hitler.

After the fall of Paris (where he was one of the last of the foreign diplomats to leave as German troops marched into the French capital) Cremin went on to serve at Vichy and continued to build up a network of contacts and informants. His talent and professionalism as a diplomat for the Irish government was demonstrated by his courageous reporting of the plight of Jewish refugees during the war and he provided an eyewitness account of the fall of Hitler's Third Reich.

Con Cremin, Ireland's Wartime Diplomat evaluates the career of one of Ireland's most influential diplomats, who proved the value of strong diplomatic reporting in shaping the foreign policy of any neutral nation.

Dr Niall Keogh was born in Dublin and grew up in Cork. A graduate of UCC, he has worked with the National Library of Ireland and the Irish Manuscripts Commission. He is currently lecturing in Moscow State University and in the state universities of St Petersburg and Voronezh.

MERCIER PRESS
WHAT YOU NEED TO READ

De Valera's Irelands

**Dermot Keogh
& Gabriel Doherty**

ISBN: 1 85635 414 8

The years of influence of de Valera are central to this interpretation of post-independence Ireland. De Valera has been made to shoulder personal responsibility for many of the defects in Irish society in that period. The essays in this book seek to re-examine and re-evaluate that charge.

Contributors: Owen Dudley Edwards, Seán Farragher, Dermot Keogh, Tom Garvin, Ged Martin, Caitriona Clear, Brian P. Kennedy, John McGahern, Brian Walker, Gearóid Ó Crualaoich, Gearóid Ó Tuathaigh and Garret FitzGerald.

Professor Dermot Keogh is Head of History at University College Cork. He is a graduate of UCD and received his PhD from European University Institute, Florence. One of the foremost authorities on the history of modern Ireland, his other interests include labour history, Church-State relations and Latin America.

Gabriel Doherty is a lecturer in the Department of History, University College Cork. He received his BA in Modern History from Oxford University and his MA from University College Galway. His principal specialities are the history of modern Ireland and Northern Ireland and the history of crime and punishment.

MERCIER PRESS
WHAT YOU NEED TO READ